Mediat[illegible]
Worl[illegible]

This pocketbook was written by
Alex Bevan, Guy Hollebon and
Samuel Passow

CRONER

Wolters Kluwer (UK) Limited
145 London Road
Kingston upon Thames
Surrey KT2 6SR
Tel: 020 8247 1175

Published by
Wolters Kluwer (UK) Limited
145 London Road
Kingston upon Thames
Surrey KT2 6SR
Tel: 020 8247 1175

First published August 2004

British Library cataloguing in Publication Data. A CIP Catalogue Record for this book is available from the British Library

ISBN 1 85524 683 X

Printed by Clays Ltd, Bungay, Suffolk

PREFACE

For employers, their employees are ordinarily the most important resource of their business, and contented employees are likely to be the most productive. For employees, their employment affords not merely a source of income and means of family support, but also their sense of self-worth. Quality of life for an employee requires a harmonious balance between the demands of the home (and family) and the demands of the workplace and a readily available and effective means of resolving any differences at the workplace.

The **Employment Act 2002** is family-friendly legislation which sets out (1) to improve the quality of life (and most particularly family life) of employees by reducing the stress which arises from employment disputes through new mandatory disciplinary and grievance procedures, and (2) to harmonise the demands of home and workplace by recognising and protecting employees' rights to maternity, paternity and adoption leave and flexible working rules. The social policy evident in the legislation is both to reduce the occasions for employment disputes and to provide alternative means of resolving those that do arise and, in particular, to place a limit on the number of cases which need to reach the overstretched tribunal system.

This valuable and handy guide aimed at human resources and line managers looks carefully at how the legislation and the new procedures in force in October 2004 will affect employers and employees and how they may best be implemented. Of particular interest and value is the part of the book that focuses on how the relatively new legal technique of mediation can be used both before and after a tribunal case is brought. The civil justice system has recognised the important role of alternative dispute resolution, and most particularly mediation, and courts may impose sanctions (in particular in respect of costs) on parties who unreasonably fail to have recourse to them. Mediation is a particularly valuable tool where there is a prospect of a continuing relationship between the parties. Mediation is not a panacea nor is it appropriate in all cases: cost, proportionality and other considerations must be taken into account. But there is increasing scope for mediation in the field of employment. Internal mediation, using impartial "wise people" with no axe to grind, at almost no cost and avoiding the damage to relations occasioned by an adversarial approach, can leave the protagonists unscarred, willing and able to get on together with their working lives.

The authors are to be commended for linking an important legislative change to a process that has become accepted as sensible and commercial. Mediation is the way forward and those who promote its practice and those who practise it are performing a valuable service to those who have need for the resolution of their disputes and to society generally.

Sir Gavin Lightman
Royal Courts of Justice
London
July 2004

AUTHORS

Alex Bevan,
senior partner of Bevans Solicitors, is a lawyer who handles all aspects of employment law, dealing with contentious and non-contentious matters. He is a founder director of ADR Group (one of the two main providers of commercial mediation services and training in the UK with 80 large national solicitor member firms) and the author of *Alternative Dispute Resolution*, published by Sweet & Maxwell in 1992. He has acted and advised in over 100 mediations on a wide range of complex commercial and corporate disputes and is ranked in *Chambers and Partners* as "a guru in employment-related mediations".

Guy Hollebon
is a partner at Bevans Solicitors with extensive experience of all aspects of employment law. He advises and represents both senior and high level employees and employers on matters including unfair dismissal, breach of contract, equality and discrimination issues, the transfer of undertakings and redundancies. Guy is an accredited mediator with ADR Group and has acted and mediated in numerous employment disputes. He took part in the first-ever online mediation pilot which involved parties in the UK and US and has been involved as a mediator in a mediation pilot scheme for a large organisation dealing with complaints. He has also delivered training on employment law issues including the use of mediation to resolve employment disputes and mediation techniques.

Samuel Passow
is a Harvard-educated international financial journalist, crisis management specialist and an experienced mediator who for the past 30 years has written and lectured extensively on analysing complex negotiations, mediation techniques and how businesses can deal with corporate terrorism. A former Head of Research for the ADR Group, and Research Associate for the Harvard University Centre for Business and Government, his articles have appeared in *The Wall Street Journal, The New York Times, The Australian,* the *Financial Times, The Times*law section and *The Guardian.* He has lectured on mediation at the University of Amsterdam Law Faculty, the Council of Europe, the American Bar Association and the Chartered Institute of Arbitrators in the UK. He is currently working on a research project for the United Nations Conference on Trade and Development.

Bevans Solicitors
is a Bristol-based progressive law firm with a national client base offering specialist advice on a wide range of commercial matters to both businesses and individuals. Bevans, which recently opened a London office, has been acknowledged for its legal expertise by both *The Legal 500* and *Chambers and Partners*.

Contents

INTRODUCTION

New employment laws in the United Kingdom and the European Union are changing the landscape of the workplace and are redefining the rights and responsibilities of both employers and employees. These new laws are a reflection of the changing social attitudes of our society.

However, it is often a lack of understanding of these changes that leads to conflicts in the workplace. How you deal with these conflicts will often show up in the balance sheet in the form of higher legal spend, insurance costs and a shortfall in revenue, as a result of lower productivity.

This guide is meant to provide a quick reference for managers and others to some of the major changes in employment law that will take place over the next five years and some of the expectations it will place on them. It is also meant to be a thought starter through discussion of innovative ways to approach forthcoming changes. Most importantly, in dealing with employment problems, we want to show where money can be saved, and offer guidance on how it should be spent properly when required.

The guide examines the present and near future of employment law in this country, paying particular attention to conflict in the workplace which, in part at least, has developed from the great range of new laws and regulations in this field. It looks at the present employment tribunal system and then moves onto the relatively new field of mediation, the purpose of which is to bring about a resolution of this conflict without any formal decision-making process being imposed. Finally, we take a short look at contractual issues. The contract itself, with its attendant policies and procedures, if well drafted, can limit conflict and assist in the resolution of problems when they do arise.

CHAPTER 1

The Changing Landscape

Conflict in the Workplace

Let us start our discussion with a brief examination of the notion of conflict. Conflicts are simply a fact of life. They are neither intrinsically good nor bad. They will occur any time two or more people interact. They cannot be eliminated, but can be managed. The results of conflict can be either positive or negative, depending on the attitudes people bring to their disagreements. Since so much of life is a self-fulfilling prophecy, coming into conflict thinking only of failure or blame leads directly to failure or blame. On the other hand, starting the process of conflict with the belief that it will lead to something good points the way towards creativity and success, and can make it a catalyst for change.

Resolving conflicts in the workplace takes time and energy, but it is certainly preferable to the alternative: no resolution. The cumulative effect of problems that are ignored or unresolved is the gradual decline into inefficiency, poor morale and even business failure. On the other hand, successful conflict resolution increases overall effectiveness, improves morale and keeps business competitive.

In April 2003, large parts of the **Employment Act 2002** came into force. One of its key aims is the reform of employment tribunal procedures and workplace dispute resolution mechanisms in response to the rising number and cost of employment tribunal claims in recent years. The figures behind this reasoning are shocking.

- By 2002, employment tribunal claims peaked at 130,000 a year: a rise of 50% over the previous three years.
- 64% of applications to employment tribunals came from employees who had not tried to resolve the dispute directly with the employer.

- The cost to business of employment tribunals has risen by 50% in just two years.
- In 2001, individual complaints to employment tribunals about discrimination in the workplace rose by 21% compared to the previous year — from 14,543 to 17,657.
- Fines for companies in work-related accidents rose 40% in 2002.
- The average fine for health and safety cases was £12,194 in 2002.
- The average fine for a work-related death in 2002 was £25,000.
- The Health and Safety Executive won convictions in 84% of cases it brought against employers.

Some may take the cynical view that the Government's main rationale for reforming the employment tribunal procedures and workplace dispute resolution mechanisms is little more than a cost-saving exercise. However, it can be seen as a move away from a blame and claim culture back to the values of self-reliance and acceptance of responsibility.

A free marketer will tell you that businesses cannot prosper if their profits are constantly eroded by the corrosive elements of regulation and litigation. Yet at the same time, society will never reap the rewards of its hard work if the dignity of labour is not preserved. A balance must be struck. The responsibility for finding that balance is now being placed squarely back on the shoulders of business. This guide advocates a proactive approach to dealing with conflict in the workplace. It looks to the progressive managers who seek options instead of seeing obstacles and to self-confident people who recognise that problem-solving requires empowering parties to come to the negotiation table.

The Spectrum of Dispute Resolution

In constructing a model for dealing with employment disputes, we find it helpful to visualise the spectrum of the dispute resolution processes that confronts every manager. As you can see in Chart 1, disputes lend themselves to three possible outcomes: negotiated outcomes, recommended outcomes and imposed outcomes. The darker the shade, the more adversarial the process becomes and the less control we have over outcome.

In an ideal world, if two people have a dispute, they meet face-to-face and work it out. When that is not possible, they call in professional negotiators, such as lawyers, to act on their behalf. When professional negotiators reach an impasse they have three options, each requiring the involvement of a neutral third party.

- A **mediator** who will facilitate a discussion between the parties so that they can reach their own solution.
- An **expert** who will recommend a solution to the parties.
- An **arbitrator, tribunal chairman** or **judge** who will impose a decision on the parties.

In this spectrum, negotiation and mediation are the most confidential and informal ways of resolving disputes. As illustrated by Chart 2, the time frame for accomplishing these tasks is a matter of days and weeks. Outcomes in zones one and two can take weeks or months and in the third zone, it becomes a matter of months and years. The darker the shade, the more formal and expensive, and of course public, the process becomes.

Chart 1 — Spectrum of dispute resolution

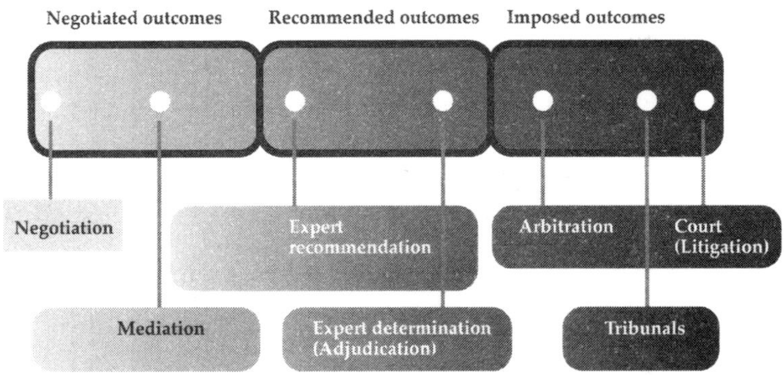

Conflict can also be measured in terms of heat. A cool conflict that can be negotiated or mediated is more likely to result in a repaired or renewed relationship — what some refer to as a win-win situation. In the work environment, this means a minimum of disruption and loss of productivity. Once a dispute goes into the third zone, to an employment tribunal or court, it becomes a win-lose situation where one party's reputation is damaged and the relationship is severed. This is a hot conflict.

A progressive manager will recognise that a cool conflict is a low-risk situation with a high degree of probability concerning the outcome. This is because, by choosing to mediate or negotiate, the manager has control over the outcome. For example, mediations in the UK have an 80%

Chart 2 — Settlement time of disputes

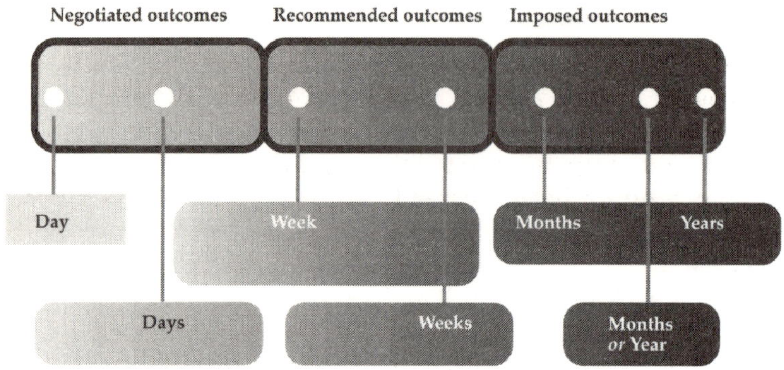

success rate, which means that both parties can engage in the process with the high expectation that they can reach an outcome they can live with. A hot conflict, with an imposed solution, is usually no more than a coin toss or 50/50 call. You can never safely predict how a judge will rule. A hot conflict may well be necessary, but it should always be a last resort.

The new dispute resolution mechanism for resolving conflicts in the workplace is due to come into force on 1 October 2004. All disciplinary issues and grievances that arise after 1 October must be dealt with in accordance with the new procedures outlined in Chapter 2.

Getting it Right from the Start

All businesses, of whatever size, strive for greater operating efficiency in order to maximise returns. An effective workforce is an important part of this. This involves not only ensuring that you employ the best people for the job in the first place, but also that there is an ongoing process of reviewing and appraising their performance. It is important to make sure that they are channelling their time and energy into their work and not being diverted away from it.

Conflicts and disputes are examples of diversions. The process for ensuring an effective workforce and therefore for saving money involves a number of stages.

It starts at the recruitment stage. You must have a clear idea of what you are looking for, what skills and experience are important to the job. Will you want that person to acquire new skills and to develop and be promoted?

The second stage in saving money for the business by avoiding costly and damaging conflicts is by making sure that staff have proper contracts of employment. The contract is an easy way to clearly define the rights and responsibilities of employees and employers. A well-drafted contract that is tailored to the particular business will avoid arguments about, for example, commission payments or holiday entitlement.

Conflicts can also be avoided by having in place clear policies and procedures dealing with important parts of your business. These should be contained in a staff handbook and may include, for example, the use of e-mail and the Internet, or guidelines to guard against inappropriate language or behaviour.

The third stage is by knowing the law. Employment law is now very complex and it is difficult for a business to stay on top of what needs to be done. The **Employment Act 2002** brings in new rights and obligations that must be understood and applied. Added to this, the influence of European social policy is increasing, and there are European directives and regulations that need to be understood.

The fourth stage is about how conflicts are approached and dealt with by the business and by individual managers. All too often in our experience they are not dealt with properly and minor problems often escalate into major differences between employee and employer. Ultimately this can lead to employment tribunal or court action. We believe that part of the progressive manager's role in leading and motivating his or her team is recognising potential conflicts and taking steps to manage and resolve those conflicts before they escalate further.

The contract of employment will help to avoid conflicts in the first place but it should also provide a mechanism for highlighting and addressing problems at an early stage. The **Employment Act 2002** brings in new compulsory statutory grievance procedures that employees and employers must use before starting a claim in an employment tribunal. As of October 2004, all employment contracts must clearly explain these procedures. The three-step statutory grievance procedures (see Chapter 2) act as an early warning system for employers of employee complaints, but the burden is still on the employer to deal with the problems effectively.

The **Employment Act 2002** also brings in new compulsory disciplinary procedures that must be used. As with the new grievance procedures, the disciplinary procedures are staged and are designed to help managers to properly exercise their authority without the constant fear of retribution or litigation. We will look at these in Chapter 2.

In January 2003, the Government accepted the recommendations of the Employment Tribunal System Taskforce (ETST), which place a greater emphasis on the prevention of disputes by encouraging the promotion of mediation schemes within companies as part of their development of internal grievance and disciplinary systems. The Government has issued revised guidelines for disputes to be heard before the employment tribunals.

One of the aims of this guide is to educate progressive managers and business owners about how internal mediation works and how it can save money by avoiding costly and time-consuming disputes, especially as it need not involve lawyers and their fees.

While well-run businesses should try to minimize costs, there will also be occasions where it is necessary to spend money in order to deal with workplace disputes. In these cases it is important that money is spent to the best advantage.

When a dispute cannot be resolved internally, it still must be dealt with. These options, however, will require a legal spend. At this point in the conflict, sound legal advice on the merits of the case and the tactics to be adopted in order to resolve the case as quickly and cost effectively as possible is a requirement, not a luxury.

Going back to the spectrum of dispute resolution in Chart 1, the darker the shade, the higher the legal costs. External mediation is a progressive manager's next line of defence. The ripeness of a case for mediation is dealt with in Chapter 5. Mediation will involve spending money on the mediator's fees and for lawyers to represent and advise you at the mediation. The costs of this need to be weighed against the higher costs of trial, the risk of paying compensation and the additional management time involved in preparing for trial and having managers out of the office for a day or more at the tribunal.

If external mediation fails to resolve the problem, it must be defended in a tribunal or a court. Again, there are dos and don'ts that managers should be aware of in preparing their case.

The key to preparing for tribunals is … preparation. Know your facts. This involves having all the paperwork, e-mails and historical facts ready and understood. It involves considering the history and analysing it carefully against the arguments in the case.

Do:

- prepare
- check that witnesses will stick to their story
- look at your opponent's arguments carefully.

Do not:

- ignore professional advice unless it is plainly wrong
- underestimate your opponent
- behave unreasonably (or you might get a costs order against you).

A final comment on spending money wisely. In order to have an effective system of internal mediation or in-house conciliation you will need to train the selected internal mediators in the proper communication and conflict-resolution skills. It is not a role for amateur psychologists or well-meaning agony aunts.

CHAPTER 2

What The Employment Act 2002 Means For You

The **Employment Act 2002**, or as the Government liked to refer to it, the "family-friendly" working Bill, mostly came into effect in April 2003. Its key themes are the enhancement of statutory rights designed to help parents balance work and family commitments, the equal treatment for fixed-term employees and the reform of employment tribunal procedures and workplace dispute resolution mechanisms in response to the rising number and cost of employment tribunal claims in recent years.

In this chapter, we will set out to explain the main provisions of the Act through the eyes of "average" employees and employers. We will try to remove as much of the legal and legislative jargon as possible so that it becomes easier to understand the core elements of the changes that will take effect in the workplace.

It is important to note at the start that the new rights given by the Act and described in this chapter (paternity leave and pay; adoption leave and pay; maternity rights; flexible working requests; statutory disciplinary and dismissal procedures; and statutory grievance procedures) apply to employees only. They do not cover self-employed contractors or "workers" in a wider sense. Chapter 6 explains how to tell whether someone is an employee or self-employed.

Paternity Leave

Twenty-five years ago giving birth and raising a family was almost exclusively a woman's domain. Pat was lucky that her husband, Chris, was allowed to leave work half an hour early to see her in hospital after she had given birth to their first child, a baby girl named Amy. At the time, even this allowance was seen as quite progressive. Now, while giving birth still remains the woman's domain, the raising of the family is increasingly being seen as a shared responsibility between mother and father. This change in roles not only affects the family environment, but the dynamics of the workplace as well.

Even when Amy was born, the **Sex Discrimination Act 1975** meant that Pat could not be sacked or refused employment because she was pregnant. Since that Act though, there have been few changes to the law surrounding raising a family and employment. Indeed Chris had to be happy with seeing Amy for 10 minutes each night when he got home from work before she went to bed. As he said, "This is just how things are." But now he says, "That was how things were."

In May 2000, in the midst of a new Mayor taking control over London, the Northern Ireland Peace Process hanging in the balance and a major summit meeting taking place in Lisbon which would open the doors of the European Union to 10 new countries, Prime Minister, Tony Blair, was off work on paternity leave following the birth of his son, Leo.

This is certainly the most high-profile example of how far we have come since 1975. In 1999, fathers were given the right to take up to 13 weeks' unpaid parental leave.

This marked a sea change in our social policy. It is no longer an issue of maternity rights. Now it is parental rights. New Labour has been influenced by a policy of equality for men and women, but underlying that is a policy that promotes the traditional family unit. The **Employment Act 2002**, which came into force on 6 April 2003, continues this policy with the introduction for the first time of the right for fathers to take paid paternity leave.

Amy has now grown up and is starting a family of her own with her husband, Bob. Bob works for a garden design company, Alpha Limited. What are Bob's rights to paternity leave and pay?

Paternity Leave Rights

- Up to two weeks' paternity leave can be taken.
- To qualify, Bob must have been continuously employed by Alpha Limited for 26 weeks ending with the week immediately preceding the 14th week before the expected week of childbirth.
- Bob must notify Alpha Limited of his intention to take paternity leave at the latest by the 15th week before the expected week of childbirth.
- Paternity leave can only be taken in one block. So if Bob takes two weeks they must be consecutive.

- Bob must take his paternity leave during the first 56 days after the birth.
- Bob can claim Statutory Paternity Pay (SPP) for this period.
- To be entitled to SPP Bob must give Alpha Limited a self-certificate form confirming that he will be taking paternity leave 28 days before he wants the SPP to start.
- SPP is currently paid at the rate of £102.80 per week (reviewed on an annual basis in line with inflation) or 90% of Bob's weekly earnings if this is less than £102.80.
- Alpha Limited can recover SPP. They deduct the amount from National Insurance contributions. In certain circumstances an employer can apply for advance funding.
- Alpha Limited must keep records of the SPP paid for three years after the end of the tax year in which Bob is paid SPP.
- Bob is also entitled to take an additional 13 weeks' unpaid paternity leave.

While Bob is taking his two weeks' paternity leave, his contract of employment remains in place and the same terms and conditions apply (except relating to pay). This means that if all staff of Alpha Limited are given an extra two weeks' annual leave while Bob is on paternity leave, he is also entitled to this. Likewise, the restrictions and confidentiality clauses in Bob's contract remain binding on him.

When Bob returns to work, it must be to the job in which he was employed before his absence. Any changes to his status, benefits or other entitlements would mean Bob could bring an employment tribunal claim against Alpha Limited. If the change is of a fundamental nature, such as affecting his salary, this could entitle Bob to resign and claim constructive dismissal.

If Bob is dismissed for a reason connected with the fact that he took or sought to take paternity leave, then this will be automatically considered unfair dismissal and Alpha Limited would face paying compensation of up to £55,000 (subject to annual increase each February).

The right to take paid paternity leave will have a financial impact on all companies. The Government estimates the costs to UK employers of implementing these new rights will be an initial £10 million outlay with recurring administration expenses of £7 million to £13 million. The costs of covering paternity leave absences are estimated at £1 million to £1.5 million.

Paternity rights apply to the partner of the birth mother, not only to the biological father. In a same-sex relationship, this would be a woman. Whoever claims these rights must also expect to have responsibility for the upbringing of the child.

Further Points to Consider

- What will happen to fathers who have left the mother and who are perhaps seeking contact with the child through the courts?

  If the contact issue has not been determined at the time that the employee wishes to take the leave, then our experience leads us to believe that in such cases, the employee will *not* be entitled to leave as the expectation of responsibility for the child should be determined at the time the father wants to take the leave.
- What if Bob wants to take the two weeks' leave to go on holiday with his mates, perhaps with, but probably without, the blessing of Amy?

  He still satisfies the criteria for the leave as the regulations do not state the purpose of the leave and therefore Alpha Limited could not refuse the leave. Of course, in this case, the sanction against Bob for misusing the right would be to incur the wrath of Amy. Perhaps Bob would be wise to think twice.
- Could a man keep forming liaisons with heavily pregnant ladies to get more time to spend on the golf course?

  We are sure that one day this will be tested in court. Like all legislation, its interpretation by judges will ultimately conform to the accepted norms of society. So over time, it is not inconceivable for courts and employment tribunals to offer different interpretations as to whether the biological father is the partner of the mother. Or of how serious the relationship must be for a non-biological father or woman to be considered a partner. However, it is our belief that the rights in this legislation encourage conformity to the traditional family unit and are strongly underlining marriage as the best way to start a family.

Adoption Leave

As with paternity leave and pay, the new rights to adoption leave also reveal a strong undercurrent of a wider social policy influencing employment legislation. In giving rights to adoptive parents that are equivalent to the rights given to birth mothers and fathers, there is a clear encouragement to adopt. This could be viewed simply as a way to increase the number of children placed for adoption each year by making adoption more appealing to prospective adoptees. Or there may be a distinct drive for adoption, rather than a scientific approach, to be the first route for a couple who cannot have children themselves.

Since April 2003, adoptive parents have had the right to adoption leave and pay equivalent to maternity provisions; in other words, up to 26 weeks' paid leave plus a further 26 weeks' unpaid leave. Before April 2003, adoptive parents only had the right to take unpaid parental leave of 13 weeks.

If Amy and Bob choose to adopt then one of them can take adoption leave. Reinforcing stereotypes, Amy chooses to take adoption leave. Amy works at Beta Brothers Greengrocers. Bob has the same rights to paternity leave and pay as if Amy had given birth, with a few minor changes over the times when the leave can be taken. What will Amy be entitled to?

Adoption Leave Rights

- Twenty-six weeks' Ordinary Adoption Leave (OAL) provided she has at least 26 weeks' continuous service with Beta Brothers at the time she is notified by an adoption agency that she and Bob have been matched for adoption.
- She can start the leave on the day the child is placed for adoption or on a date no more than 14 days before the date the child is expected to be placed with them.
- Amy must give notice to Beta Brothers within seven days of being notified of the adoption placement or as soon as reasonably practicable after that and must tell her employer the date the child is expected to be placed with her and Bob and the date on which she wants to start adoption leave.
- Beta Brothers can ask for this notice to be given in writing.
- Within 28 days of receiving Amy's notice, Beta Brothers must write to Amy stating her expected date of return.
- During her period of OAL, Amy is entitled to the benefits of her terms and conditions of employment that would have applied if she had not been absent, except for terms and conditions relating to remuneration. If Beta Brothers gives all staff company cars then Amy is entitled as well. Amy also remains bound by her obligations to Beta Brothers, such as confidentiality and not working for competitors.
- There are specific rules to cover the circumstance where the adoption is disrupted, for example because the placement has been ended or the child dies.

- Amy does not need to give notice of her return from OAL unless she wishes to return early, in which case she must give 28 days' notice.
- Amy is entitled to return from OAL to the job in which she was employed before her absence, with the same seniority, pension rights and other rights as she would have had if she had not been absent.
- After her Ordinary Adoption Leave Amy could take Additional Adoption Leave (AAL) for a further 26 weeks.
- When she is on AAL, Amy is entitled to the benefits of Beta Brothers' implied obligation of trust and confidence and to any terms and conditions relating to notice of termination, compensation in the event of redundancy and disciplinary and grievance procedures. In return, she remains bound by her obligation of good faith to her employer.
- Whether Amy remains entitled to other benefits such as company car, mobile phone and health-club membership depends on her contract with Beta Brothers. Chapter four deals with this in more detail; however, her employer would be wise to have a clear Adoption Leave Policy specifying whether benefits and perks will continue through AAL.
- After her period of AAL, Amy has the right to return to the job she was employed in before her leave or, if that is not reasonably practicable, to another job which is suitable and appropriate in the circumstances.
- Amy has no obligation to give notice of her return from AAL unless she wants to return early, in which case she must give at least 28 days' notice.
- While she is on OAL or AAL Amy has the right not to suffer any detriment. If this happens she can bring a claim in the employment tribunal. If she is dismissed for a reason connected to her adoption leave this is automatically considered as unfair dismissal.
- So long as Amy has at least 26 weeks' continuous service with Beta Brothers she can elect in writing to receive Statutory Adoption Pay (SAP). She must give Beta Brothers at least 28 days' notice of the date she wishes to start receiving SAP.
- SAP is available for 26 weeks.
- It is paid at the rate of £102.80 per week or 90% of Amy's normal weekly earnings if these are less than £102.80. In short, the maximum that Amy can receive is £102.80 per week.
- The employer can recover SAP through National Insurance contributions.

The impact of these rights on Beta Brothers may be quite substantial. It will need to arrange for cover for Amy and when Amy wants to return, possibly a year later, there may be no job for her to do. The person covering could have accrued one years' continuous service and therefore to dismiss him or her may lead to an unfair dismissal claim. On the other hand, Beta Brothers knows that the rules contain an exemption that a dismissal is not automatically unfair if the employer has less than five employees and it is not reasonably practicable to allow Amy to return to a suitable and appropriate job. Beta Brothers must still act fairly and reasonably in all the circumstances and this would mean that there must be a genuine reason why Amy cannot return. Beta Brothers must not be motivated by bad faith and use this as a way to get her out. Her employer should also consult with Amy and explore whether there is any alternative employment for her.

Regardless of the number of staff it has, if Beta Brothers has a genuine redundancy situation whilst Amy is on adoption leave then this can be a fair reason not to take Amy back. They must still consult with her and act fairly and reasonably in the circumstances. Also, if there is suitable alternative work available then Amy is entitled to be offered it.

A Further Point to Consider

- Unlike childbirth, there are no time delays between children when adopting. Therefore, Amy and Bob could adopt in January. They could then adopt another child in March. What happens to Amy's entitlement to paid adoption leave?

We suggest that adopting in March extinguishes the earlier entitlement so Amy starts again from March. This situation could also apply if Amy and Bob adopt and while Amy is on adoption leave she becomes pregnant. Again, we would suggest that the birth would start maternity leave and extinguish adoption leave.

Maternity Leave

It is not just fathers and adoptive parents that have the **Employment Act 2002** to thank for new rights. Mothers have also been given additional rights. Maternity leave and protection to pregnant women from dismissal is something that has been in place for some time. In fact, it was these rights that allowed Pat to keep her job when she had Amy's younger, and unexpected brother, Richard. Pat relied on the right to take maternity leave and received Statutory Maternity Pay (SMP). She then returned to work. In fact, by the time of Richard's birth, the idea of a father being more involved in bringing up the family was starting to spread and Chris was given the day off after Richard's birth. This was unpaid and he had to make it up the following Saturday, but this was still viewed as progressive at the time.

Maternity leave and the precise details about when it starts, what notices need to be given and when they must be given are incredibly complex. Not difficult *per se*, just difficult to follow the detail. When dealing with maternity rights issues refer to the *Reference Book for Employers*, and use the online Employment Ready Reckoner on the Croner website (*www.croner.co.uk*) to make maternity calculations. For further information go to the Department of Trade and Industry website (*www.dti.gov.uk*) which has an online guide to maternity rights or *www.tiger.gov.uk* (Tailored Interactive Guidance on Employment Rights) where you can access information on maternity, paternity and adoption rights and flexible working policies.

The **Employment Act 2002** seeks to strengthen a woman's maternity rights. So, what can Amy now expect to receive from her employer, Beta Brothers?

Maternity Leave Rights

- Ordinary Maternity Leave (OML) of 26 weeks, provided that in or before the 15th week before her expected week of childbirth she notifies Beta Brothers of her pregnancy, her expected week of childbirth and the date on which she expects her OML to start.
- If Amy has at least 26 weeks' continuous employment with Beta Brothers at the week before the 14th week prior to the expected week of childbirth she is entitled to Additional Maternity Leave (AML) of a further 26 weeks after the OML period.
- Statutory Maternity Pay (SMP) for a period of 26 weeks. Amy will receive 90% of her normal weekly earnings for the first six weeks and thereafter be paid at the current rate of £102.80 per week. Amy must give her employers at least 28 days' notice of the date from which she expects SMP to commence.
- Beta Brothers can offset payments of SMP against sums due to the Inland Revenue. They can also apply for advance funding of SMP.

As a mother can now claim an entitlement to one year off work, and possibly longer if she gives birth again or adopts a child within that one year period, employers may be taking on maternity cover for over a year. This means that the person employed as cover may build up enough continuous service to claim unfair dismissal.

For example, Beta Brothers decides to take on Gita as cover for Amy. Gita works there for over a year. When Beta Brothers realises that Amy is returning they tell Gita that her services are no longer required. Gita must be given contractual notice and, as she has over one year's continuous service, she can claim unfair dismissal. Beta Brothers needs to act very carefully and consult with her and consider alternative employment. On the other hand, if it dismisses Amy, she has an automatic unfair dismissal claim.

In fact, employers can avoid this tricky problem. What Beta Brothers should have done was give Gita written notice at the time of recruitment (not when she actually started) that the job is to cover maternity leave and that her employment will be terminated when Amy returns. This avoids the risk of Gita bringing an unfair dismissal claim.

A growing number of medium to large-sized firms already recognise the push towards greater family-friendly working practices and they embrace this. They have a career break scheme aimed at mothers that allows them to have a career break in order to care for children.

If you already have a scheme like this, or plan to start one, there is an important contractual obligation to consider. If the career break scheme does not break continuity of employment then in any later redundancy situation, your employee will receive a payment based on all her years with your company including those during which she was on the break scheme. The policy must be worded very carefully to make it clear that the scheme brings her employment to an end, but that there is a guarantee to re-employ when she wishes to return. It would also be wise to put a long-stop deadline for her return to work. If continuity of employment remains then the employee will be entitled to receive payment for four weeks' holiday per year even if she receives no other payments during the year.

Case Law 1

Curr v Marks & Spencer [2003] IRLR 74 CA

The employee took advantage of Marks & Spencer's career break scheme and took four years off work. When she returned to work she was made redundant. Marks & Spencer calculated her redundancy payment based on service since the career break. She argued that her continuous service dated back to when she first started at Marks & Spencer, before the career break. The Court of Appeal held that the career break did not maintain her continuity of employment. In reaching this decision it relied heavily on the wording of the policy that referred to "re-employment".

As maternity leave and pay are not new creations there are a lot of cases concerning these issues. The provisions are complex and proper advice should be sought. Interestingly, the aim is to prevent pregnant women and women who have had babies from being treated unfairly in their employment. However, in giving women these rights it may have had a different effect, as businesses, and small businesses in particular, may decide not to employ women in the first place so as to avoid having to give them these rights.

Of course, the **Sex Discrimination Act 1975** outlaws this, and an employer who does not employ women at all, or women of child-bearing age, runs a very high risk of a sex discrimination claim. There does not have to be direct evidence of discrimination, and in most cases there will not be. Employment tribunals can infer discrimination based on surrounding facts. So long as a woman can show that she has been treated differently and less favourably, there will be a finding of sex discrimination unless the employer can show a reason for the decision that is unconnected to sex. Compensation for sex discrimination is unlimited, so an employer who does decide not to employ women for fear that they will be entitled to maternity rights will be running a very high financial risk.

Flexible Working Rules

Just after Amy was born Pat and Chris were chatting about whether Pat should try and get a job once Amy was older. Pat said that it would be ideal if she could choose her own hours to fit in with looking after Amy and being there when she got home from school. She imagined a world where she could work hours that suited her life style and not just nine to five. Pat and Chris laughed. By the time that happens, they joked, people would be holidaying on Mars and shopping on the Moon.

Now, Pat's "pie in the sky" fantasy is coming true, in part at least. The **Employment Act 2002** contains the right for an employee to request family-friendly and flexible working practices. This is the cornerstone of the Government's family-friendly policy and aims to encourage a greater work-life balance. But bear in mind, while the employee is allowed to request these rights, the right of the employer to reasonably refuse such a request is equally protected.

Amy and Bob now have a son called Ian. Amy has been on maternity leave and her additional maternity leave period is due to expire shortly. She has decided not to opt for the Beta Brothers career break scheme, as she needs the income from work. However, she doesn't want to work standard hours because of her childcare responsibilities.

There are various options for Amy. These include working practices such as:

- **Flexitime** — you are obliged to work x hours per week and you have core hours where you must be at work. Outside the core hours it is up to you when you work, provided that you do the required number of hours.
- **Compressed hours** — you are required to work, say, 20 hours a week. Rather than five hours a day you compress your work into two or three days.
- **Homeworking or teleworking** — people work from home, this will usually be task driven and the worker chooses his or her own hours.
- **Job-sharing** — the work of a full-timer is undertaken by two part-timers sharing that role.
- **Term-time working** — you only work when the children are at school and you are then free during school holidays to care for the children.
- **Shift working** — working on a set cycle which changes periodically.
- **Staggered hours** — you work different hours each day, week or month. For example, one week you work two days, the next week you work four days.
- **Annualised hours** — like flexitime but you have an annual target of hours and it is, in the main, up to you when you do them.
- **Self-rostering** — again, you choose the hours you work, usually to fit in with your colleagues.

The right to request a contract variation does not just apply to Amy. Bob can also make a request to Alpha Limited. Under the **Employment Act 2002** the employer must consider a request by either a man or woman in the following circumstances.

- The employee must have 26 weeks' continuous service to make a request.
- The mother, father, adoptee, guardian or foster parent of the child can make a request. Someone who is married to such a person and living with the child, or is the partner of such a person, may also make a request. This includes same-sex couples.
- The purpose of the request is to enable the employee to care for a child. No other purpose can be considered.
- Only employees who care for children under six or care for a child with a disability under 18 can make a request.

- The request must be in writing (this includes e-mail), must state whether a previous request has been made and provide details of that request and must be dated.
- The request must also specify the change applied for and the date on which it is proposed the change comes into effect.
- The employee must also set out what effect, if any, he or she thinks the change will have on the employer and must set out any thoughts on how to overcome such effects.
- The employee must also self-certify that he or she and the child meet the qualifying conditions for making the request.
- Having made an application, the employee cannot make a further one for 12 months.
- If the employer agrees to a change, this will be permanent, unless otherwise agreed. Once Ian reaches six years old, the changes to Amy and Bob's contracts will not be affected.

Employer's Obligations Upon Receiving a Contract Variation Request

- The employer must hold a meeting to discuss the request within 28 days. A longer time period can be agreed between employer and employee, in which case this should be recorded in writing and signed and dated by both the employer and the employee.
- The employee has a right to be accompanied to the meeting by a trade union official or a fellow worker.
- There is no need for a meeting if the employer agrees to the contract variation and notifies the employee within 28 days of the request.
- We suggest that the employer must have an open mind during the meeting, or at least be seen to have this. In practical terms, this means not making a decision until after the meeting, making sure that the employee has the opportunity to put forward all of his or her points about the requested contract variation. The employer should also test out the employee's theories. In other words, if the employer has doubts over the viability of a key member of staff only working part time, it should say so, explaining the business or operational reasons for this view. It must, however, be stressed that this is not the final decision, merely an initial thought.

- After the meeting, the employer should consider carefully the points made by the employee. If it is likely that the decision will not be accepted readily by the employee, then a brief file note stating the thought processes could be made.
- Within 14 days of the meeting, the employer must provide notice of its decision in writing and this must be signed and dated.
- If the decision is not to allow the contract variation, the notice must set out the grounds for refusal (see below), must contain a sufficient explanation as to why those grounds apply and must set out the appeal procedure for the employee.
- An employee is entitled to appeal the decision by giving notice within 14 days of the date on which the decision notice is sent to him or her. The notice of appeal must set out the grounds for appeal and be signed and dated.
- Within 14 days of receiving notice of appeal the employer must arrange an appeal hearing. At the appeal hearing, the employee again has the right to be accompanied.
- Finally, within 14 days of the appeal hearing the decision must be sent in writing to the employee.

Grounds Upon Which a Request Can Be Refused

- Burden of additional costs.
- Detrimental effect on ability to meet customer demand.
- Inability to reorganise work among existing staff.
- Inability to recruit additional staff.
- Detrimental impact on quality.
- Detrimental impact on performance.
- Insufficiency of work during the periods the employee proposes to work.
- Planned structural changes.

The request can only be refused on these grounds. Employers should consider the matter carefully and not mislabel or make up reasons.

Example Refusal

Dear Amy

I am sorry that I cannot grant your request to leave at 3.30 pm each day, as this will severely affect our ability to meet customer demand and I am unable to cover your absence. You are currently the only authorised signatory that works at the end of the day and it is essential that we are able to load the lorries and sign them off for overnight deliveries. Due to the fact that we supply perishable goods (fruit and vegetables) it is not possible to load the delivery lorries any earlier in the day. I have spoken to the two other authorised signatories and they are presently unable to change their hours. I also advertised in the local paper and in the job centre when Leanne left, but could not find anyone to cover her job. As this was only two months ago, it is not appropriate to go through the process again now.

If an employer fails to hold a meeting to discuss the request, fails to give notice of its decision, or fails to provide an employee with a right of appeal, the employee can complain to an employment tribunal. Also, if an employer rejects a request based on incorrect facts then the employee can go to the employment tribunal. Any claim must be made within three months of the breach.

The tribunal is not looking at whether it would have made that decision. It is simply looking at whether the procedure was followed and whether a decision to reject was on one of the specified grounds and was based on reasonable information. Therefore *as long as the procedure is right and the employer has given a reasoned explanation of the decision, it will not be criticised by the tribunal.*

If a complaint is upheld, the tribunal may order the employer to correct the procedural defect and/or make an award of compensation. The amount of compensation is that which the tribunal considers to be just and equitable in all the circumstances but is capped at a maximum of eight weeks' pay, where a week's pay is itself capped (currently at £270).

It is automatically unfair if an employee is dismissed because of making a request. Also the employee must not be victimised because of making a request.

When making and dealing with requests the forms can be found in *Croner's Personnel in Practice (Records and Procedures)*. The DTI have also produced recommended forms to use.

When dealing with requests, employers must be careful to act fairly and reasonably and not to discriminate against people. If one member of staff has been allowed to alter his or her working hours and another identical request is refused, there must be a genuine reason for this not based on sex, race or disability. We would advise employers to have a clear policy on dealing with requests. For example, you may only be able to accommodate one or two changes, in which case this should be spelt out to all staff so that it does not come as a shock to them later on and give them the excuse to say, "But she was allowed to change her hours and leave early."

Case Law 2

Chief Constable of Avon and Somerset Constabulary v Chew EAT/ 503/00

Ms Chew was a police officer who wished to work part-time in order to help her with childcare arrangements, as she was a single mother. The police force had a policy that employees could work part-time on a shift rota system. Ms Chew could not work on a rota system as this meant that she would not have the same days at home each week and she could not make childcare arrangements to fit in with the changing shifts. She wanted to work fixed part-time hours. The force's policy applied to all staff that wished to work part-time, however, fewer female officers could comply with the requirement than male officers. The employment tribunal found that this amounted to indirect sex discrimination.

As this is such a new right for employees, there will undoubtedly be aspects that the courts and tribunals will need to define. Some of the possible problem areas as we see them are as follows.

- It is quite common for a member of the extended family to help with childcare arrangements. Perhaps an aunt or grandparent has primary responsibility while the mother and father go out to work. The aunt or grandparent may even live in the same house as the child. As they have significant childcare responsibility, can they request a change to working hours? The answer appears to be no. While they may have responsibility for the upbringing of the child and live in the same household, they are not a parent or the spouse/partner of the parent.

Of course, if the aunt or grandparent has adopted the child or is their legal guardian, then they will have the right.

- As with paternity leave, rights are given to the partner of the mother/father. What degree of relationship will be required to constitute a partner? The definition of partner means someone who lives with the child's mother, father, adoptee or guardian and there must be an "enduring family relationship". The underlying social policy is to reinforce the traditional "happy" family. What about an unmarried couple who cannot afford to live together in their own place and live apart with parents? The man may be the most supportive father figure but will be denied the right to request flexible working practices.
- The request for a contract variation must be for the purposes of caring for a child. What does this actually mean? If a man wants to work part time, but his daughter goes to a nursery or school, is this request for the purpose of caring for a child? He may not be physically caring for his daughter when he is at home as she is at the nursery but he is tidying her room or making her supper and so caring for her indirectly. What if he takes a break when she is at the nursery and does something for himself?

We think that there is no clear way to answer these questions. Much will depend on the surrounding circumstances. However, the ultimate decision will fall to an employment tribunal. Therefore, as well as dealing with workplace issues as industrial juries, tribunals must also be alive to issues of childcare. Will they get additional training on this? Will a white, middle-aged, middle-class male tribunal member be best qualified to say what constitutes childcare? From our considerable experience of employment tribunals, we think that it may take some adjustment, but we hope they will be able to deal with these issues. But there is always the rogue tribunal.

Dismissal, Disciplinary and Grievance Procedures

The number of employment tribunal claims has increased dramatically in recent years. In part this is due to increased work-place rights and a greater awareness of and willingness to use those rights. It is also because employers may not have appreciated that an employee was feeling so strongly about a particular issue. On a more complex level, employment legislation, and more particularly how it is interpreted, has become increasingly procedural in recent years. There has been a distinct shift by employment tribunals in the last six years to a culture where procedure is king and the ultimate fairness and, if there is such a thing, justice plays out a submissive closing act. Unfortunately for employers, the procedures were not written down in stone and were the preserve of lawyers together with a few enlightened mere mortals.

The **Employment Act 2002** recognises this shift to procedural law and in fact defers to the process by setting out statutory procedures that must be followed when disciplining or dismissing an employee and when an employee raises a formal grievance. The procedures cover disciplinary and dismissal procedures (DDPs) and grievance procedures (GPs) which are commenced after 1 October 2004.

The Government has issued regulations **(The Employment Act 2002 (Dispute Resolution) Regulations 2004)** that provide more details of how the DDPs and GPs will work in practice. The draft regulations state that the DDPs and GPs will apply to all types of dismissal (including conduct, capability, redundancy, retirement and the expiry of a fixed-term contract) and to actions short of dismissal such as suspension without pay and demotions. Importantly, they will not apply to oral or written warnings where it is intended that the GPs should be invoked by the employee if appropriate.

For many employers, and employees alike, the new procedures could easily be seen as just additional hoops to jump through before they can have their day in court. But there is another way to view the new statutory procedures which is explained in Chapter 5.

Effect of the Procedures

When the DDPs and GPs come into force from October 2004 there will be an initial trial period during which the procedures will not be deemed to be incorporated into contracts of employment. Nevertheless they must still be adhered to because the rules about preventing employment tribunal actions and increasing and decreasing compensation if the procedures are not adhered to will apply. Existing procedures that go over and above the DDPs and GPs will still apply. The statutory procedures are minimum standards. Following them will not, by itself, prevent an unfair dismissal claim.

Employers are already obliged to provide employees with a written statement of their terms and conditions of employment within two months of starting work. Now, this written statement must contain details of the procedure that will be followed if the employee is to be disciplined or dismissed. Alternatively, the written statement must refer the employee to a readily accessible document containing the procedures, for example a staff handbook.

If an employee is successful in a claim for, among other things, unfair dismissal or discrimination and as part of that successful claim it becomes apparent that the employer has not provided adequate written particulars, then the tribunal must award a minimum of two weeks' pay and may award four weeks' pay in addition to the compensation for the unfair dismissal or discrimination. A week's pay is currently capped at £270.

Employers should review their existing contracts and amend them if appropriate to avoid this.

The Procedures Explained

The steps that must be taken are explained below. Each step and action under the procedure must be taken without unreasonable delay.

The timings and location of meetings must be reasonable. Meetings must be conducted in a manner that enables both the employer and employee to explain their cases. Does this allow an employee or an employer to argue an entitlement to legal representation at the Step 2 meeting or the Step 3 appeal? We think that this could only be the case where the particular issues were complex and perhaps where there were technical legal arguments that the individual or employer could not reasonably be expected to explain properly.

The Regulations and guidance provide no indication of what will be a "reasonable" period of time between Step 1 and the Step 2 meeting. Ultimately this will be a matter for the tribunals to determine. We would suggest that each case will be different and will depend on factors such as the complexity of the issues surrounding the alleged conduct and how serious the possible consequences are. We would suggest that in general terms, allowing an employee five working days would be reasonable.

Where it is reasonably practicable, a more senior manager than dealt with the Step 2 meeting should run the Step 3 appeal meeting.

The modified two-step DDP will be used very infrequently and will apply in cases of serious misconduct leading to dismissal without notice where it was reasonable for the employer to dismiss without notice. The Regulations do not explain when it will be considered reasonable to dismiss without notice, nor do they explain who decides the reasonableness.

The modified GP is to be used in cases where the employee has already left work, for example where they have resigned and are claiming constructive dismissal, and the employer was unaware of the grievance before the employment ended or was aware of it but the standard procedure had not been started, or not finished, before the employee's last day of employment. Both parties must agree in writing that the modified procedure should be used.

The modified procedures would also be appropriate in cases where the employee has been subjected to harassment and has not wanted to complain while still employed and so has found another job, resigned and is then raising the harassment, provided that both the employee and the employer agree in writing to use the modified procedure.

The modified DDP does not involve a meeting taking place between the employer and the employee. This is because it is only to be used in the most exceptional cases where the conduct is so serious and blatant that instant dismissal, with no disciplinary hearing, is appropriate.

Neither grievance procedure will apply if the subject of the grievance is the employee's dismissal or contemplated dismissal. In this case the employer will follow the DDP and the employee can raise concerns as part of the DDP. In addition, neither grievance procedure will apply if the employee has left work before a grievance procedure was commenced and since leaving it is not reasonably practicable for the employee to provide a Step 1 statement.

Standard Dismissal and Disciplinary procedure

Step 1

Statement of grounds for action and invitation to meeting

- The employer must set out in writing the employee's alleged conduct or characteristics, or other circumstances, which led him or her to contemplate dismissing or taking disciplinary action against the employee.
- The employer must send the statement or a copy of it to the employee and invite the employee to attend a meeting to discuss the matter.

Step 2

Meeting

- The meeting must take place before action is taken, except in the case where the disciplinary action consists of suspension.
- The meeting must not take place unless:
  - the employer has informed the employee what the basis was for including in the statement under Step 1 the ground or grounds given in it, and
  - the employee has had a reasonable opportunity (see above) to consider his or her response to that information.
- The employee must take all reasonable steps to attend the meeting.
- After the meeting, the employer must inform the employee of his or her decision and notify the employee of the right to appeal against the decision if he or she is not satisfied with it.

Step 3

Appeal

- If the employee does wish to appeal, he or she must inform the employer.
- If the employee informs the employer of his or her wish to appeal, the employer must invite the employee to attend a further meeting.
- The employee must take all reasonable steps to attend the meeting.
- The appeal meeting need not take place before the dismissal or disciplinary action takes effect.
- After the appeal meeting the employer must inform the employee of his or her final decision.

Modified Dismissal and Disciplinary Procedure

Step 1

Statement of grounds for action

- The employer must set out in writing:
  - the employee's alleged misconduct that has led to the dismissal
  - what the basis was for thinking at the time of the dismissal that the employee was guilty of the alleged misconduct, and
  - the employee's right to appeal against dismissal.
- The employer must send the statement, or a copy of it, to the employee.

Step 2
Appeal
- If the employee does not wish to appeal, he or she must inform the employer.
- If the employee informs the employer of his or her wish to appeal, the employer must invite the employee to attend a meeting.
- The employee must take all reasonable steps to attend the meeting.
- After the appeal meeting the employer must inform the employee of his or her final decision.

Standard Grievance Procedure

Step 1
Statement of grievance
- The employee must set out the grievance in writing and send the statement or a copy of it to the employer.

Step 2
Meeting
- The employer must invite the employee to attend a meeting to discuss the grievance.
- The meeting must not take place unless:
  - the employee has informed the employer what the basis for the grievance was when he or she made the statement under Step 1 above, and
  - the employer has had a reasonable opportunity (see above) to consider his or her response to that information.
- The employee must take all reasonable steps to attend the meeting.
- After the meeting the employer must inform the employee of his or her decision as to his or her response to the grievance and notify the employee of the right to appeal against the decision if the employee is not satisfied with it.

Step 3

Appeal

- If the employee does wish to appeal, he or she must inform the employer.
- If the employee informs the employer of his or her wish to appeal, the employer must invite the employee to attend a further meeting.
- The employee must take all reasonable steps to attend the meeting.
- After the appeal meeting the employer must inform the employee of his or her final decision.

Modified Grievance Procedure

Step 1

Statement of grievance

- The employee must set out in writing:
  - the grievance, and
  - the basis for it.
- The employee must send the statement, or a copy of it, to the employer.

Step 2

Response

- The employer must set out his or her response in writing and send the statement, or a copy of it, to the employee.

Failure by an Employee to Comply with DDPs and GPs

Barring of Employment Tribunal Claims

Where an employee is under an obligation to use a statutory GP, he or she is prevented from making a claim to an employment tribunal unless he or she has complied with Step 1 of the GP.

Even when Step 1 has been complied with, an employee must wait 28 days from complying with Step 1 before lodging any tribunal claim. This will not apply where the grievance is raised by someone who has already left employment.

Reduction in Compensation

If an employee is successful in a claim in the employment tribunal but the statutory DDP or GP had not been completed before the proceedings were begun and the non-completion was caused by the employee not complying with the statutory DDP or GP or not appealing, then the tribunal must reduce any award of compensation by between 10 and 50%.

The reduction is compulsory unless in exceptional circumstances it would be unjust or inequitable.

Example 1

Alpha Limited employs Amy. She has been subjected to sexual harassment from a colleague. She brings an employment tribunal case. The tribunal bars her claim as she has not complied with Step 1 of the GP as she has not given Alpha Limited a statement of her grievance. The next time it occurs, Amy makes a formal complaint and gives Alpha Limited a Step 1 statement. Alpha Limited tries to arrange the Step 2 meeting with Amy but she refuses to attend. 28 days after sending the Step 1 statement, Amy commences employment tribunal proceedings for sexual harassment. She is successful and is awarded £10,000 compensation. As the failure to comply with Step 2 was Amy's fault, the tribunal must reduce her compensation by 10-50%.

Example 2

Amy is then accused of dishonesty although there is no evidence to support this. Alpha Limited provides a Step 1 statement of grounds for action, arranges a meeting with Amy and informs her of the decision to dismiss her. Alpha Limited then gives Amy details of the appeal procedure but she declines to appeal. Amy has over one year's service and commences an unfair dismissal claim. She is successful, although, as she didn't appeal the decision, her compensation will be reduced by 10-50%.

Example 3

Amy suffers further sexual harassment and decides to leave Alpha Limited because a better job comes up. She does not claim constructive dismissal. A few days after she has left, she raises a formal grievance under the modified procedure for former employees and sends Alpha Limited a Step 1 statement. Alpha Limited does not respond.

Amy commences employment tribunal proceedings. She is successful in the tribunal claim and is awarded £10,000 compensation. As the failure to comply with Step 2 of the modified GP was Alpha Limited's, the compensation is increased by 10-50%.

Example 4

Alan has worked for Delta Limited for five years. He is called in to his manager's office one day and told his performance is not up to the job and he is dismissed with a payment in lieu of notice.

Delta has not complied with the statutory DDP and the dismissal is automatically unfair. Additionally, Alan's compensation must be increased by 10-50%, as it was the employer's fault that the DDP was not complied with.

Example 5

Ben also works at Delta Limited. He has been there two years and is now suspected of theft (in this case we assume he is guilty) and is given a statement of the grounds for action under Step 1 of the DDP. Delta Limited then arranges a meeting under Step 2, and afterwards informs Ben that he is to be dismissed. He will be paid in lieu of his notice entitlement.

Ben informs Delta Limited that he wants to appeal. Delta Limited does not see any use in this, as Ben was guilty and refuse to arrange an appeal hearing. As the DDP has not been followed by Delta Limited it is automatically unfair dismissal. There may be arguments about the amount of compensation but the dismissal remains unfair.

Failure by an Employer to Comply with DDPs or GPs

Unfair Dismissal

If an employee is dismissed and the relevant statutory DDP has not been complied with through the fault of the employer, this will amount automatically to unfair dismissal. The employee must still have at least one year's continuous service to claim this.

If an employer complies with a statutory DDP, any dismissal may still be unfair, either because the employer's decision to dismiss was not based on a genuine belief of guilt on reasonable grounds following a reasonable investigation, or the decision did not fall within the range of reasonable responses that a reasonable employer would have made.

If an employer has its own disciplinary procedures that go beyond the limited scope of the statutory DDPs then a failure to follow its own procedures would not be automatically unfair, provided that the statutory procedures had been complied with, as a minimum. For example, an employer's procedures may involve at least two meetings with the employee before a dismissal. In this case, so long as one meeting is held (the Step 2 meeting in the DDP) and the employer can show that it would have decided to dismiss regardless of whether there had been a second meeting, the dismissal will be fair, assuming that there is a substantively fair reason for the dismissal (such as genuine misconduct).

Increase in Compensation

If an employee is successful in a claim in the employment tribunal but the statutory DDP or GP had not been completed before the proceedings were begun and the employer's non-compliance with the statutory DDP or GP caused the non-completion, then the tribunal must increase any award of compensation by between 10% and 50%.

The increase is compulsory unless in exceptional circumstances it would be unjust or inequitable.

When the DDPs and GPs Need not be Followed

The Regulations provide that neither party has to follow the statutory procedures when one of the following conditions exists:

- Either the employee or the employer has reasonable grounds to believe that following the DDP or Grievance Procedure would result in a significant threat to themselves, their property, any other person or the property of any other person
- Either the employee or the employer has been subjected to harassment and has reasonable grounds to believe that following the DDP or GP would result in further harassment. The Regulations define harassment and make it clear that the test is an objective one. Therefore, while the perception of a party that they were harassed will be a factor to be considered it will ultimately fall to the employment

Chart 2 — How tribunal decisions and awards are made

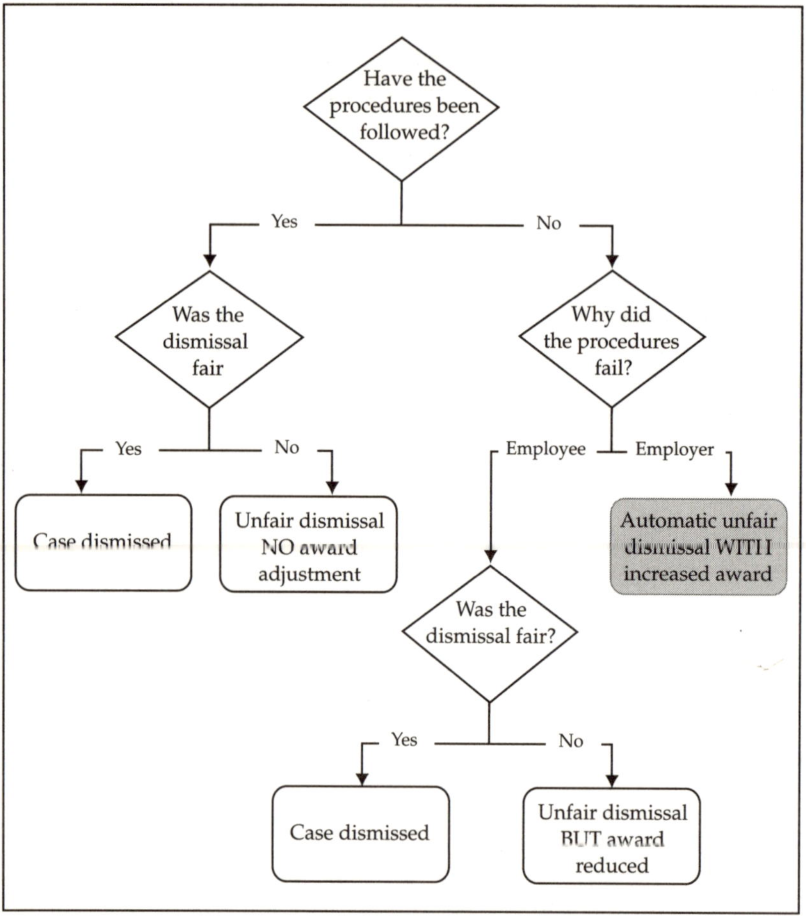

Source: DTI
Guidance on the Employment Act 2002 (Dispute Resolution) Regulations 2001 and associated provisions in the Employment Act 2002

tribunal to determine whether conduct amounted to harassment. We feel that stress or anxiety will not be sufficient to amount to harassment.

- It is not practicable for either the employee or the employer to follow the DDP or GP within a reasonable period.
- The issue is being discussed "collectively".

- The employee applies for "interim relief".
- To follow the procedures would require the disclosure of information contrary to the interests of national security.

In addition to the above, the DDP will not apply where:

- the employer dismisses a group of employees but offers to re-engage them on or before termination of their employment. This is frequently used as a last resort to impose new terms and conditions of employment — staff are sacked and offered re-engagement on the new terms
- there are collective redundancies and the employer consults with employee representatives
- the employer's business closes down suddenly because of an unforeseen event and the employer does not employ any employees any longer
- the employee is no longer able to work because they are in breach of legal requirements, eg to hold a valid work permit.

There are also detailed circumstances where even though the DDP or GP has not been followed or completed, the parties shall be treated as having complied with the procedure. The effect of this will be that neither party will be penalised for failing to comply.

Further Points to Consider

Cooling-off Period

Once an existing employee makes a Step 1 statement of grievance there is a 28-day bar on going to an employment tribunal. What if the employee was concerned that vital evidence would be destroyed in the 28-day embargo period and the tribunal could not be involved? The 28-day bar only applies to commencing employment tribunal proceedings. Therefore the employee could seek an emergency injunction to preserve the vital evidence from the High Court.

The above point is an extreme example. In the normal course of events, the 28-day period acts as a "cooling off" period and prevents knee-jerk claims in the tribunal. As explained in Chapter 5, this cooling-off period may present an opportunity for a clever and progressive employer to use alternative dispute resolution methods and to allow the parties to talk before they become entrenched in adversarial employment tribunal action.

Time Limit

An employee must commence an employment tribunal claim within three months from the act complained of. However, the new Regulations specify certain situations where the three months can be extended to six (see below). The employee will be barred from going to the tribunal if he or she has not complied with an applicable statutory GP. The claim will be struck out only if it is apparent from the application that the GP has not been followed or if the employer raises the argument.

There will be a revised tribunal application form that will ask whether the GP has been followed. If the tribunal does not pick up on the failure by the employee to follow the statutory GP, it might pay, as an employer, not to raise the issue until the tribunal hearing date. If this is later than six months from the act complained of the employee's claim cannot proceed and they are outside the time limit for starting fresh proceedings.

There are three circumstances where the normal three-month time limit for starting employment tribunal proceedings will be increased to six months. These are as follows.

1. If the employee has complied with Step 1 of the GP before the normal time limit for presenting a tribunal claim and before presenting their claim to the tribunal.
2. If the employee has presented a complaint to a tribunal within the normal time limit but it is rejected because the GP has not been followed or the employee has not waited for the requisite 28 days.
3. Where, at the end of the normal three-month time limit, the employee had reasonable grounds for believing that a DDP was ongoing. In order for this to apply there must be genuine discussions still taking place between the employer and employee and at the end of the normal time limit the employee had reasonable grounds for believing that a DDP was ongoing.

Contractual Rights

In due course the DDPs and GPs will be deemed to be part of all employees' contracts of employment, and a failure to follow them will amount to a breach of contract. Therefore, if they are not followed, any restrictions on working for competitors or taking clients will not be enforceable.

At present, an employee with 11 months and 20 days' service who is dismissed without any procedures having been followed and who is paid in lieu of notice will not be able to commence unfair dismissal procedures as they do not have one year's service. When the new statutory procedures are contractual, that employee may be able to argue that if the contract had been complied with, the procedures would have been followed and by the time this would have been done, the employee would have gone over the one-year service mark.

Case Law 3

Virgin Net Limited v Harper [2003] IRLR 831

This concerned an employee who was dismissed shortly before the one year anniversary of the commencement of her employment, without being given her contractual notice period. Had she worked her contractual notice period she would have gone over the one year's service required to claim unfair dismissal. The employee argued that her claim for breach of contract should include damages for the loss of opportunity to claim unfair dismissal on the basis that had the contractual notice been given she would have been able to claim. The Employment Appeal Tribunal overruled an earlier case and held that damages for breach of contract could not include the loss of opportunity to claim unfair dismissal.

It seems to us that this case may be tested and overruled when the DDPs and GPs are made contractual.

Senior Executives

The new DDPs and GPs apply to all employees, including senior executives. At present it is unusual for a senior director to be put through formal disciplinary proceedings. More likely, the decision will be taken and the parties will then negotiate. The introduction of the new procedures will give senior executives additional bargaining powers in circumstances where the decision is taken without the procedures having been followed.

- Restrictive covenants may be rendered unenforceable and the senior executive will only agree new ones if additional consideration is given.
- The failure to comply with the DDP by the employer will mean the tribunal increases any award by at least 10%.

Therefore, the senior executive could argue that the package offered to him or her should be increased likewise. For employers, we think that any offers put to a senior executive, or indeed any staff member, in circumstances where the statutory procedures have not been followed, should be expressly stated to take this possible uplift into account.

Constructive Dismissal

Does a failure by an employer to follow the contractual DDPs and GPs amount to a fundamental breach that would entitle the employee to resign and claim constructive dismissal? This is especially important, as a failure by an employer to follow the DDP or GP is automatically unfair. If an employer did not follow the GP procedure, could the employee resign and automatically claim unfair constructive dismissal? Initially the answer will be no, as the DDP and GPs will not be contractual. However, when the Government decides to deem them incorporated into all contracts of employment we think that a breach would be a breach of a fundamental term of the contract of employment, entitling an employee to resign and claim constructive dismissal. However, we also think that the tribunal would not support an employee who sets out to engineer such a claim and even if they were unfairly dismissed, we think that their own contributory conduct would reduce any compensation dramatically.

Employee Does Not Attend a Step 2 or Step 3 Meeting

If the failure to attend the Step 2 or Step 3 meeting was for a reason that was not reasonably foreseeable at the time the meeting was arranged, the meeting must be re-arranged. Examples that would be reasonably foreseeable would be sudden illness, car breakdown or unexpected childcare arrangements.

The employee will not be penalised for failing to comply with the DDP and the employer is obliged to invite the employee to a further meeting. If the meeting fails for a second time due to unforeseeable reasons neither party will be at fault and the parties will be treated as having complied with the DDP.

If the employee fails to attend and gives a reason which could be foreseen then they will be at fault and could have any compensation they may be awarded reduced.

CHAPTER 3

The View From Brussels

The Human Rights Act and EU Employment Directives

In 1992, John Major, as UK Prime Minister, negotiated an opt out from the Maastricht Treaty Social Chapter. The opt out permitted this country to take the slow lane for laws and regulations protecting individuals in the workplace and in society. Europe went ahead and legislated in areas such as working hours, health and safety, rights of dismissed workers and consultation with workers over the running of enterprises. Major wanted to give Britain a chance to be more competitive in a less regulated workplace. He succeeded for a while but things moved on.

There are strong arguments that a sound social policy backed by good regulations is good for society and ultimately for the economy. It might be felt though that the balance went too far towards a single, cross-border social policy in the instance of Maastricht and that to some extent John Major may have protected UK employers by his opt out in 1992.

Many of the concepts that underpin the **Employment Act 2002** have their origins in European social policy. In particular, the strong move towards family-friendly working practices and increased rights for mothers, fathers and adopters. Countering this move towards a workers' rights based system are the provisions aimed at cutting the number of employment tribunal cases. "You can have more rights, but we will make it harder for you to assert them before an employment tribunal".

The influence of continental Europe in our employment regulation will not lessen, with increased rights for part-time workers, fixed-term workers, temporary agency workers and older workers.

In part, these rights will complement the rights granted by the **Employment Act 2002**. As employees make use of the new right to request more flexible working practices, then the law must develop to make sure they are not disadvantaged in doing so. For example, if part-time workers were not entitled to pro rata pay and benefits as full-time workers, employers would simply state that part-time staff would receive lower pay and less benefits. Even with the right to request part-time work, who would, or could afford, to do so?

The Human Rights Act 1998

Perhaps the greatest impact that any European law has had on our employment rights is the European Convention on Human Rights.

The **Human Rights Act 1998** (HRA) is a major piece of legislation passed by Parliament to give effect in the UK to rights and freedoms guaranteed under the European Convention on Human Rights. The HRA represented for the UK a move out of the slow lane and into the fast lane of European law. The specific rights are set out in Schedule 1 to the HRA which refers to the Articles as set out in the European Convention.

The HRA has importance in connection with a number of areas of employment law:

- The giving of references (Article 1)
- The right to a fair trial (Article 6)
- The right to respect for private and family life (Article 8)
- Freedom of thought, conscience and religion (Article 9)
- Freedom of expression (Article 10)
- Freedom of assembly and association (Article 11)
- Prohibition of discrimination (Article 14).

The Act specifically applies to public authorities such as local authorities, health trusts, universities and the police, but it has much wider implications for private employers.

How Does This Law Work?

The HRA guarantees the right to a fair trial which includes the right to:

- a fair hearing
- an independent and impartial tribunal
- a hearing within a reasonable time.

Example 1

Nurse Cripps is a male nurse working in a mixed ward at the local general hospital. A young girl of 14, a patient in this ward, alleges that he indecently assaulted her. The administrator in charge interviews the girl in a long and persistent way, frequently asking leading questions such as, "When he put his hand under the bedclothes, did you say ...?", instead of simply asking what happened next. The administrator then interviews Cripps without prior warning. Cripps is suspended and an internal tribunal is convened. The same administrator takes charge of the disciplinary process. The administrator chairs a panel that meets 12 months later. Cripps' lawyer is not allowed to cross question the girl. The disciplinary panel decide that Cripps did commit the assault and he is dismissed for gross misconduct. The Nursing and Midwifery Council takes its own disciplinary proceedings, two years later, and these are still continuing. But Cripps is unable to get a job because the reference from his previous employers mentions the assault — as it must do.

In Example 1, these rights appear to have been seriously breached. It wasn't fair to interview the child in a leading manner; it wasn't fair to see Cripps without warning him what the interview was about; the tribunal was not impartial as the administrator was the chief investigator and 12 months is an unacceptable delay when memories fade fast.

It has come to light that the girl was in care and had a documented history of false complaints about men, including her father and brother. Both the police and social services knew her. The unfair and delayed procedures failed to uncover the true facts and led directly to an injustice. A witness who knew about the girl's history of fantasies of assault left the hospital a month after the episode and was unavailable for the final hearing.

Both the internal procedures of the health trust and the giving of the reference could give rise to claims against the trust under the HRA and substantial damages could follow. For the loss of a career a court can award well over £100,000. Employment tribunals can award well over £50,000.

Tip: Make sure, particularly if you are a public authority, that your contracts and investigatory and disciplinary procedures comply with the HRA as well as the Employment Act 2002 (see Chapter 2).

Respect for Private and Family Life

This is an area of increased interest for government, public authorities, employers and the individual. The events of 11 September 2001 have heightened the debate over the *right to privacy* set against the *right to interfere with privacy* in order to safeguard national interest (listening devices in mosques would have been unthinkable only a few years ago) and protect economic wellbeing or prevent crime. This debate has an impact in the field of employment.

Example 2

Christine Halford was an assistant chief constable who was in dispute with her employers. They surreptitiously monitored her calls using their own equipment and during working hours at the office. This was found to be unacceptable and in breach of Article 8 of the European Convention on Human Rights. After a fight taking her to the European Court of Justice she received substantial damages for the interference with her human right to privacy.

On the other hand, this right is not unqualified and the HRA envisages circumstances where the protection of the rights and freedoms of others may permit interference with the right to privacy. For example, in a case where there are grounds to suspect an employee of theft, it may be acceptable to conduct some form of surveillance.

It is an interesting contrast to see how French law dealt with this situation. An employee was caught on closed-circuit television taking a large denomination note out of the till and stealing it. He was sacked immediately. He took the employer to the equivalent of an employment tribunal. It decided that the surveillance was in breach of his right to privacy and not only awarded compensation but also reinstated the man. It is not known what happened to the francs he stole!

Surveillance affects the workplace in a number of ways:

- e-mail checking
- monitoring phone calls
- telephone tapping
- computer screen monitoring
- drug testing.

The right to privacy versus the right to interfere is a question of balance.

- An airline pilot has no right to insist on privacy about his or her intake of alcohol or drugs while he or she is in command of the plane.
- A senior police officer cannot have his or her phones tapped to discover matters about his or her personal affairs (including the

conduct of his or her claim against the employer). On the other hand if there is a grounded suspicion that he or she is taking bribes from criminals, then a tap is justified.
- Anti-pornography interception of e-mail is right, but is it appropriate for personal, but inoffensive, e-mail to be censored as being not being related to work?

Tip: The best answer lies in having a clear and publicised policy in this area that complies with the HRA and all other employment law and achieves this balance of privacy without interference with morals and the rights and freedoms of others.

Freedom of Assembly and Association

The HRA provides for freedom of expression without interference from public authorities. Employees should be able to say what they think. This includes making disclosures of matters of public interest in connection with the activities of the employer. Whistleblowers who make an appropriate disclosure in the right way can expect protection from Article 10 of the European Convention on Human Rights.

Is this right of free expression unlimited? The answer is not at all. It is recognised that some occupations such as teaching and the civil service require a counterbalancing duty of moderation. At the very least they must refrain from expressing their views in the workplace. However, a teacher named Ms Vogt was successful in challenging a dismissal on the basis of her membership of an extremist party despite the recognition of the need for moderation.

Religion and Prohibition of Discrimination

The right to freedom of thought, conscience and religion does not extend to a refusal by the employer to allow time off for religious purposes, since that refusal adds up to enforcing contractual hours. A claim would need to be on the basis that somehow an employer was preventing an employee from practising his or her religion. The balance is quite fine and more similar cases may come to the European courts.

EU Employment Directives

These are laws that the European Union set out as framework directives. They give the general content of the rules and stipulate a date by which they must be in force. It is then up to the individual Member States how they actually implement them.

The following are a selection of existing and forthcoming regulations that are likely to impact on businesses that want to promote family friendly and progressive employment practices. Only a brief outline of each of the regulations is given.

Part-time Workers

The **Part-time Workers (Prevention of Less Favourable Treatment) Regulations 2000** ensure that part-time workers are not treated less favourably in their terms and conditions of employment than comparable full-time workers. This means that hourly rates of pay should be the same for part-time workers as full-time workers.

Part-time workers should also have the same rights to sick pay, maternity and paternity leave and pay, holiday pay and access to pension schemes. Where appropriate, these rights can be on a pro rata basis. For example, Amy works two and a half days per five-day week. Her colleague Betty works five days and is entitled to 20 days' holiday a year. As Amy is a part-time worker, she is entitled to 10 days' holiday per year.

A part-time worker who has been treated less favourably than a full-time worker can claim compensation from an employment tribunal. An employer may avoid paying compensation if it can justify the treatment and can show that it is necessary and appropriate to achieve a real business aim.

The regulations apply to the wider category of "workers" and not just employees (see Chapter 4 for a discussion of the distinction). The effect is that as a business owner you must not treat part-timers less favourably even if they are self-employed and do not have tax and National Insurance deducted from their pay.

Fixed-Term Employees

The **Fixed-Term Employees (Prevention of Less Favourable Treatment) Regulations 2002** prevent employees employed on fixed-term contracts from being treated less favourably than comparable permanent employees on the ground of their fixed-term status unless it can be shown that there is an objective reason to justify such treatment.

This specifically includes the right to have the same opportunities to receive training and to have the same opportunities to secure permanent employment. In fact, a fixed-term employee has the right to be informed of available vacancies. This means that employers must ensure vacancies are advertised where the fixed-term employee has a reasonable opportunity to see them.

Objective reasons for treating a fixed-term employee less favourably might include level of skill or qualification or a difference in the work.

One very interesting point is that in determining whether a fixed-term employee has been treated less favourably, you must assess the terms and conditions as a whole. Therefore, if Amy is a fixed-term employee and her employer wishes to restrict her access to the company gym membership scheme by having a rule that only staff with six months' continuous service can join, he can do so provided that Amy is compensated in some other way such as additional pay or increased holiday entitlement.

Agency Workers

There is a proposed EU Directive covering temporary agency workers. Agency workers are supplied by the agency to the user company and work under the direction and control of the user company. It is proposed that agency workers whose assignments last longer than six weeks should not be given less favourable working time rights and pay than would apply if they had been employed directly to do the same work by the user company.

The Government is committed to protecting temporary workers as it recognizes that temporary work allows a person greater flexibility over working time and practices than permanent work and therefore sits happily alongside the flexible working rights in the **Employment Act 2002**.

Under the proposed regulations this will change. One area of concern that the Government and industry sectors have is that pay is to be covered by the Directive. This means that temporary staff must be paid the same as permanent staff. It is unclear at the moment whether this will include the same rights to pension benefits. In any case, there is a risk that legislation covering pay may actually put employers off taking on temporary staff as the benefits to the employer of temporary staff are lost.

This remains a proposal at present but watch this space.

In addition to this EU Directive, new regulations came into force on 6 April 2004 which regulate temporary and permanent recruitment. The full effects of these Regulations are outside the scope of this book. However they compel recruitment companies to agree terms and conditions with candidates and hirers before doing anything to find a vacancy/candidate. The regulations also render temporary to permanent fees unlawful unless the hirer is given a choice of paying the fee or having an extended period of hire. The Regulations are the **Conduct of Employment Agencies and Employment Business Regulations 2003**.

Case Law

Dacas v Brook Street Bureau [2004] IRLR 358

Mrs Dacas was a cleaner working for Wandsworth Council. She was a temp worker supplied to the Council by Brook Street Bureau. She was paid by Brook Street but took her instructions from the Council. The arrangement continued for four years. When her engagement was terminated she commenced employment tribunal proceedings for unfair dismissal against both the Council and Brook Street. The employment tribunal held that she was not an employee of the Council because there was no contract between them and neither was she an employee of Brook Street because, while there was a contract between them, they did not exercise day-to-day control over her work and consequently there was no employment relationship.

Mrs Dacas appealed and the Employment Appeal Tribunal overturned the original decision and said that she was an employee of Brook Street as they paid her wages, had the right to initiate disciplinary proceedings gainst her and had the right to terminate her contract.

The Court of Appeal held that Brook Street was not the employer and has hinted that in future the end user is likely to be the employer. The Court of Appeal held that the control exercised by the Council and the length of the arrangement was sufficient to create an implied contract between Mrs Dacas and the Council.

Age Discrimination

The Government is committed to introducing legislation to prevent discrimination in employment on the grounds of age by 2006 and is currently consulting on how best to do this. However, employers must not treat a person differently and less favourably on the grounds of their age.

The age discrimination legislation will recognize that differences of treatment on the grounds of age are sometimes necessary and can be justified, for example, in order to protect an employee's safety and welfare. The final legislation may also lead to the abolition of mandatory retirement ages.

Even though age discrimination legislation is not expected until 2006 we are already seeing a growing recognition by the employment tribunals of the importance of having an age-diverse work force.

Case Law 4

Secretary of State for Trade and Industry v Rutherford IRLR [2003] 858

Mr Rutherford was dismissed in circumstances that were unfair. He claimed unfair dismissal before the employment tribunal. His employers pointed out that the age limit for bringing an unfair dismissal claim is 65 and argued that he was stopped from proceeding because he was aged over 65. Mr Rutherford argued that the age limit amounted to indirect sex discrimination, as while it applied to everyone, far more men than women worked beyond 65 and therefore the age limit had a disproportionate impact on men. The employment tribunal agreed and ruled the 65 age limit to be unlawful. The Government successfully appealed the decision. Mr Rutherford has now taken his case to the Court of Appeal.

Employers should bear this in mind when dismissing an employee aged over 65. The employer should ensure that there is a genuine reason for dismissal such as conduct, performance or redundancy and a fair procedure *must* be followed too.

Sexuality, Religion and Belief

In December 2003, regulations to prevent discrimination based on sexuality and religion or belief came into force. The **Employment Equality (Sexual Orientation) Regulations 2003** mean that people in same-sex relationships must not be treated less favourably than heterosexuals. This goes hand in glove with the new rights to parental leave and adoption leave, which apply to same-sex couples.

The regulations dealing with religion or belief will be difficult to interpret when it comes to making decisions as to what defines a religion, or lack of one, or a belief. These issues are complex and a full discussion of them is outside the scope of this book.

CHAPTER 4

The Employment Tribunal System

Employment tribunals were first set up under the Labour Government in 1964. They were first used for disputes relating to training, then for redundancy cases and, in 1971, unfair dismissal was added. Then they were known as industrial tribunals, but British industry became less dominant and they are rightly now called employment tribunals (ETs) to reflect the change in the type of employment over the last forty years. They now deal with a very wide range of issues falling under the umbrella term "employment law".

Tribunals are like courts but have a culture of speed, cheapness, freedom from technicality and expertise in subject matter. ETs still have these features but the extraordinary growth of employment law has led to some complications and the speedy informality of old is not always present. It is possible, for example, for sex and race discrimination cases to last for weeks and to deal with very complex points of law. Sadly, lawyers have crept in and, over the last 20 years, started to dominate.

The whole idea was to set up a system able to offer employers and employees the best opportunity to arrive at "an amicable settlement of their differences".

One of the key ways this was and is done is through the use of the Advisory Conciliation and Arbitration Service (ACAS). This is a non-departmental public body linked to ETs, whose operatives are trained to conciliate between the parties. The use of ACAS is perhaps better known through involvement in large-scale, collective industrial disputes, such as the 2002-2003 firemen's conflict. ACAS also works effectively on the individual level, helping each side to reach settlement through conciliation ("an act of reconciling or bringing together the parties in a dispute with the aim of moving forward to a settlement acceptable to all sides").

This vast growth in employment law has, unsurprisingly, caused a great increase in applications to ETs. In 2000-2001 there were 130,408 applications. This fell the next year, largely due to a fall in multiple applications but a better guide is single applications, which did not fall greatly. Cases are also getting more complex and the trend is still for an increase in the overall workload. Tribunals are increasingly mirroring the civil courts and are now more procedurally orientated.

The Current Employment Tribunal System

This is the system for people to go through in order to enforce their rights in the field of employment. ETs are the first port of call but if aggrieved with the decision there is a right of appeal to the Employment Appeal Tribunal (EAT). However, this is on a point of law only and the ETs are the key forum for deciding the facts (what happened). ACAS is independent from the ETs but closely linked. It is part of the Department of Trade and Industry.

Employment Tribunals

There are two full-time Presidents of ETs, one in Scotland and one in England and Wales. They are lawyers. There are then regional and local chairmen who are also lawyers. They preside over the tribunal hearings and advise on the law. There are also part-time chairmen in view of the pressure on the system.

There are then Lay Members. The Secretary of State for Trade and Industry appoints them. They have experience of dealing with employment problems and there is one with an employer perspective and one with an employee perspective.

The usual panel for a tribunal is a chairman (lawyer) and two lay members (each with a different perspective). In some cases, such as breach of contract claims, and where the parties have agreed, the chairman can sit alone. Otherwise all three have an equal vote and the lawyer can be outvoted.

Location

The central office for the ETs in England and Wales is at Bury St Edmunds. There are a number of regional offices in major centres. Details can be found on the Employment Tribunal Service website *www.ets.gov.uk* or on *www.employmenttribunals.gov.uk*.

Employment Appeal Tribunal

The Employment Appeal Tribunal (EAT) is a proper court and has the same status as the High Court. It has a panel of legal members and lay members. The legal members are High Court or Court of Appeal judges. It carries a lot of weight and its decisions bind ETs. It takes an awfully long time to deal with any but simple cases — because of overload. When judgments do come, they are heavyweight and bear careful attention.

ACAS

This service offers practical independent and impartial help to employers and employees by:

- providing advice on employment relations issues and law through a national telephone helpline system
- publishing guides as to codes of practice
- running seminars and training
- working with both sides to resolve disputes both before and after applications have been made
- operating an arbitration service to save time if both parties agree
- beginning to operate a mediation service — but it is still early days.

Because it is non-departmental, ACAS does not behave like a Government department and can be very helpful and light-handed. The traditional style of its conciliation is reactive rather than proactive. This means ACAS is less likely to say, "Why don't you offer £x because you accept there is a weakness on this/that point?" It is more likely to say, "Are you interested in settling?" and if there is an affirmative response, then it will carry an offer to the other side and repeat the question as to whether there is interest in settling. Its constitution and culture of independence and impartiality has led it in this direction. This is fine, but there may also be a case for more forceful guidance towards settlement and it is now looking at mediation as a tool in the dispute resolution kit. Private organisations offer this too.

The Employment Tribunal Service Taskforce (ETST) has published a report, *Moving Forward*, which recommends that more mediation be introduced into the workplace, both through ACAS and private/commercial organisations. The ETST Report defines mediation as "Where an independent third party acts as an intermediary in talking to both sides. The aim is for the parties to resolve the problem themselves, but the mediator will make suggestions along the way". The key difference from conciliation is the pro-active intervention in this role.

Internal or in-house mediation, discussed in Chapter 5, is distinct from external mediation where an outside mediator is completely independent. Internal mediators have a bottom line loyalty to the employer. Nevertheless, this can be an effective tool, the more so if policies are in place to reinforce its use and appropriate confidentiality terms apply (see Chapter 6). These give comfort and confidence to employees that the process won't be misused.

The Future of the Employment Tribunal System

The ETST recommends that better and more widely spread information about the system should be made available. It recommends that the simplicity of the system should be maintained and that alternative forms of resolution of disputes (such as in-house or external mediation) should be used.

Inevitably, with more and more employment laws the trend towards complexity will continue. It is likely that specialist advice will be necessary in many cases. As competent managers in this field you will have to make a choice as to whether to use external advisors and representatives and, if so, which ones. This will have a big impact on (a) whether you succeed or perhaps more importantly, (b) whether you settle on sensible and commercial terms taking into account the risks in the case and the level of costs likely to be incurred (including serious diversion of management time).

A number of concerns were expressed to the ETST about aspects of advice and representation. First, that the failure to appreciate that skilled representation might be needed for the purpose of dealing with a complex claim left certain users at a disadvantage, particularly when reaching the hearing stage. "As a lay person I had understood that the tribunal system was a mechanism for resolving employment issues, a forum where legal representation was not necessary. My experience proved otherwise...".

The second concern expressed was that inequalities of representation led to an uneven approach to the resolution of a claim, which favoured highly-resourced legal firms over lay representatives, as well as unrepresented users of the system.

Third, it was felt that lack of knowledge on the part of employers, either through lack of understanding or lack of proper appreciation of their responsibilities in respect of employment rights, meant that many cases went to full hearings which, if such failures had been appreciated earlier, might have been disposed of much more quickly and efficiently. These were often inadvertent as opposed to deliberate failures on the part of employers.

The ETST recognised that some employers, having received advice, will wish cases to proceed to a full hearing, for example, where important principles are at stake. Nevertheless, research provided by ACAS suggests that only a small minority of employers wish to take a case to a full employment tribunal. Even where employers, either directly or through a representative, stated a preference for a full hearing, a significant proportion of this group of employers ultimately settled their cases through ACAS or had the claim against them withdrawn. Also, where there was a preference for an employment tribunal, represented employers were more likely than unrepresented employers to settle the claim through ACAS and conversely unrepresented employers were more likely than represented employers to have the case against them withdrawn (source: Survey of Tribunal Applications 1998).

Concern was expressed to the ETST during consultation about the activities of certain providers of legal advice. The adequacy of advice and representation given was questioned in some cases, as was the pursuit of parties by commercial organisations seeking to offer their services to uninformed parties to tribunal claims in a manner that was designed to create concern about their financial exposure. The Leggatt Review of March 2001, which reported on the tribunal system, identified similar concerns. The Leggatt Review noted that no apparent action had been taken to curb employment advisors' activities and urged the Government to reconsider the issue. The ETST endorsed these concerns. In Scotland, the Law Society of Scotland already runs a system of accreditation of specialists by a suitably qualified assessment panel. Specialist status is given to solicitors who can demonstrate expertise gained from practicing in the field of employment law and show substantial experience in that field. The ETST recommended that urgent

Chart 3 — Applicants' main reasons for settling in cases where they perceived the settlement to be unfair (%)

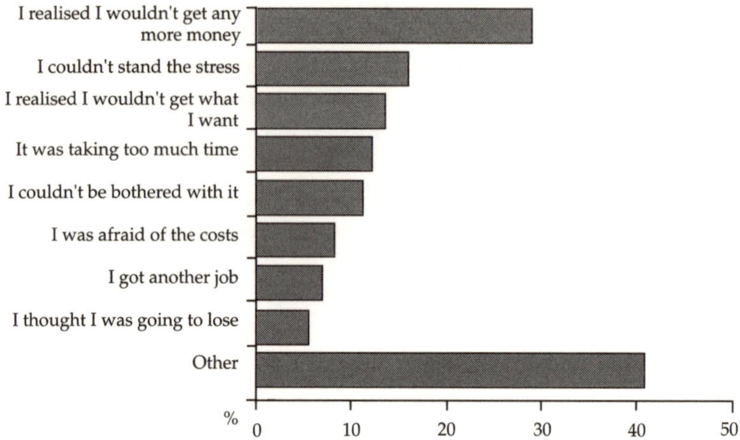

Source: Survey of Tribunal Applications 1998

Chart 4 — Employers' main reasons for settling in cases where they felt the applicant had a weak case (%)

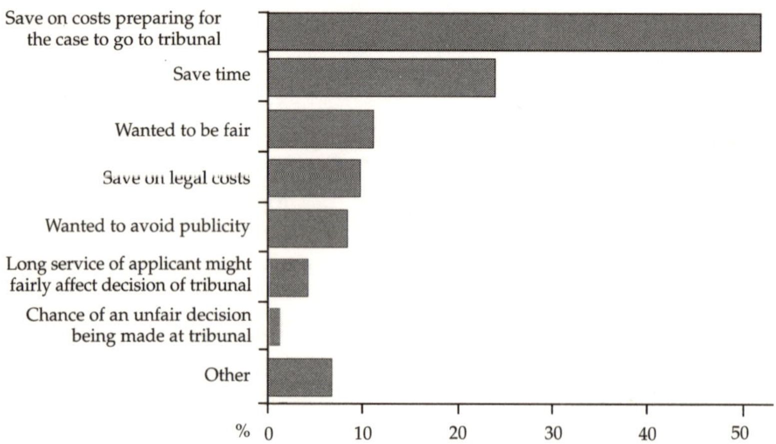

Source: Survey of Tribunal Applications 1998

consideration should be given to a review of the regulation of the providers of employment law advice, taking into account the experience of accreditation schemes already in place.

Generally, in relation to representation, the ETST believed that there should be a co-ordinated approach to directing users of the employment tribunal (ET) system to sources of advice and representation. When commencing a claim in the ET system, users should be directed to appropriate sources of help if they experience difficulties, for example, in completing the relevant form to commence a claim or filing a notice of appearance. Accordingly the ETST recommended that:

- a review be undertaken to consider the regulation of providers of employment law advice, taking into account the experience of accreditation schemes already in place.
- sources of advice should be listed and made available to users of the ET system particularly if users experience difficulties when completing application forms for access to the ET System or Notices of Appearance.

The Government has approved all the Taskforce recommendations.

In conclusion, the system will get more complex, there will be a growing need to consider whether to use specialist advice and the sources of this advice are to be monitored and accredited to ensure quality standards. Of course, if you can nip a dispute in the bud by using mediation techniques (internal or external) so much the better. The main thrust of the **Employment Act 2002** is to put resolution of employment conflict back into the hands of the participants in the workplace and so use of mediation is completely consistent with this. It can also earn brownie points if the case doesn't settle and eventually does go to a hearing.

Using the Employment Tribunal

The ET is for those wishing to protect or enforce their employment rights. There are time limits that are strictly enforced as to when the claim must be brought. With rare exceptions, the typical unfair dismissal claim must be brought within three months of the effective date of termination. In sex, race and equal pay claims there are also time limits in respect of the act or acts complained of, with three months being the most common. It pays to check carefully with an up to date employment guide, as it may be that all the pain of a complaint can be removed at a stroke if there is a failure by the applicant to comply with these limits.

Procedure

The aggrieved employee (applicant) or his or her representative goes to a regional tribunal office and issues a form IT1 known as an Originating Application. This form can also be sent by fax. It contains the key facts of employment and details of the complaint. This can later be amended by approval of a chairman (by post or at a preliminary hearing) but if there is to be a radical change and a new claim added, for example a sex discrimination claim, then normally the time limits still have to be complied with.

The regional office then sends out the IT1 to the employer (respondent), who has three weeks to respond with a form IT3, known as a Notice of Appearance. This form is the answer to the complaint and must set out the argument as to why, for example, the dismissal was fair. It should go into some detail but it is not a witness statement. This will come later. If the ET does not receive the IT3 within the time limit (it may be extended but official ET approval is needed for this), then the employer has no right to be heard at the hearing of the case. It can be seen, therefore, that time limits are critical for each party.

A chairman then looks at the papers. He or she decides if there are any automatic issues that spring out, such as time-limit failures or the case being not one the ET has the power to deal with. In such cases orders can be made at once, although there is usually the right to be heard at an interim hearing if the decision is wrong. Communication with the ET is by telephone, fax or letter. Bristol is now operating an e-mail system and can even issue online. Tribunal centres vary in speed and efficiency, but the whole system is quite congenial and user friendly. Help is given on procedural matters but not the law.

Normally, a case that gets through the first hoops and is not dismissed early will have a set of directions issued with a date for a hearing given. It is very important to notify the ET if that date is not suitable and supply good reasons. This might be that key witnesses, or you the employer, are not available then. Bearing in mind that a lot of tribunals ask for available dates before giving a hearing date, you will have to have a good explanation for the postponement and do not assume you will get it.

Other directions will involve the agreeing of a bundle of relevant documents and exchange of witness statements. Typically, the bundle is ordered in not less than 14 days from the hearing and the statements not less than seven days.

Further directions may be sought. For instance, in a more complex case there may be categories of documents that the applicant wants disclosed by the employer such as personnel file, interview notes recruitment policies and so forth. If the employee is on a fishing expedition it may be sensible to resist the disclosure application. There will be a hearing to decide this. More and more nowadays this is done by telephone to save money, with applicant and respondent having a telephone conference. In one recent case the directions order made over the telephone by the Bristol tribunal was e-mailed to both sides within an hour of it being made.

Witness Statements

Witness statements are very important. They set out the evidence that each side will rely on. They may be added to on the day of the hearing but some tribunals are fierce about limiting this scope and so you must get into the statements everything you think you will need to say. They should set out clearly in chronological order what happened and what was your thinking as an employer in making the decisions you did. Much (but not all) of employment law is about whether the employer behaved in a way that fell within the range of reasonable responses.

Ensure that your witnesses carefully read what they are "stating" before they sign. Do not pressure them to say more than they are happy with — it will end in tears as they are cross-examined back to the true position.

Before the hearing, ensure that all witnesses know where to arrive and that they are willing to come. If they are not, ask the tribunal to issue a witness summons requiring them to attend.

If you are taking legal advice, keep in touch with your lawyer about witnesses and the bundle. If not, follow the tribunal guidelines and produce a clear, logical bundle that is properly paginated and, hopefully, agreed with the applicant.

If you lose but feel aggrieved you can appeal on legal grounds, not factual ones, to the Employment Appeal Tribunal (EAT). You ought to seek proper legal advice, but remember that there are 42 days to appeal from the date the tribunal gives its decision. If the decision is delayed (reserved) the 42 days run from the date the decision is delivered. The EAT is fierce in its control of time limits and usually there is no mercy if you are late. The scope of the EAT is beyond this book, but note that normally the appellant has to make out its case before the EAT alone, before the full, two-party, hearing is convened. The aim is to cut out hopeless appeals before high costs are incurred. You may be the recipient or respondent of an appeal. It can take a year or more to process, only to be kicked out at the first stage. This is frustrating and we recommend patience in these cases.

CHAPTER 5

How To Mediate Employment Disputes Effectively

Alternative Dispute Resolution and Employment Disputes in the UK

Alternative dispute resolution (ADR) has been used in employment disputes in this country for over 100 years, dating back to 1896 when the Government set up the first voluntary conciliation and arbitration scheme. Apart from a name change or two (to the Industrial Relations Services in 1960 and the Conciliation and Advisory Service in 1972) the basic service was much the same and remained under the Government's wing.

Then in the mid-1970s, an independent council with statutory control was set up and re-branded as the Advisory Conciliation and Arbitration Service (ACAS). During the industrial unrest of the late 1970s and early 1980s (for example, the miners' strike, the dockers' walk-outs, or the battle for Wapping when Rupert Murdoch dramatically changed working practices in the newspaper printing industry), industrial mediation became more popular and the idea that people could talk through and resolve complex business problems began to take hold.

But it was the introduction of mediation as a way of resolving civil and commercial disputes by the private sector in the early 1990s that heralded a dramatic breakthrough in the use of mediation as a viable alternative to litigation. Organisations such as the ADR Group, the Centre for Effective Dispute Resolution (CEDR Solve) and the Academy of Experts campaigned hard for the inclusion of mediation as a "best practice" standard by the legal profession.

Finally, in April 1999, it was included in the Civil Procedure Rules (CPR) that were more commonly known as the Woolf reforms (named after Lord Woolf, who chaired the committee that re-wrote the 118-year-old rules of how our civil court system works). Now judges have the power to suggest to parties that they try and mediate their disputes before they litigate, taking up court time and money. Employment tribunals follow the principles of the CPR more and more.

Part of that sea change in government policy of making justice both time efficient and cost effective has now worked its way to employment tribunals. As we saw in Chapter 2, under the new Employment Act both employers and employees will have to abide by a strict three-step procedural code before they can bring a case before an employment tribunal. The reason for the change is very simple. By 2002, employment tribunal claims had exceeded 130,000 cases a year, a 50% rise in just three years. What is more shocking is that 64% of applications to employment tribunals had come from employees who had not tried to resolve the dispute directly with the employer at all. In short, the boss wakes up one morning, opens his or her post and finds out that legal action is being taken against the firm. Like our courts, the tribunal system could not cope with the volume of work, created in part by frivolous cases, and reform was desperately needed.

Mediation

By their very nature, employment disputes are not only adversarial, but are highly personal. Virtually every dispute is emotive because it directly affects someone's livelihood. This is where mediation can be a valuable management tool and, more importantly, an agent for smooth and efficient change.

In-house mediation and traditional mediation are both private and confidential processes of reconciling or bringing together the parties in a dispute with the aim of giving the parties an opportunity to resolve the problem between themselves rather than having a judgment imposed on them, as is the case in civil litigation, arbitration or in tribunal.

The main differences between the two (in-house mediation and traditional mediation) are who pays for the process, where the talks take place, the independence of the mediator, and the degree to which confidentiality can be relied on.

How In-house Mediation Works

- Talks are held privately at the workplace.
- The mediator is a company manager/non-executive director/consultant mediator chosen by the company, someone who does not have direct line-responsibility for the employee.
- The mediator initially meets each party individually and may then decide to bring the parties together.
- The mediator tells the parties whether a deal is possible and liaises over implementation of the settlement. He or she does not decide the case.
- If the case is not settled, the usual DDP/GP procedures continue.
- The process is paid for by the employer.

The three-step DDP/GPs (see Chapter 2) are basically an adversarial process because all they require an employee to do is to signal intent to lodge a formal complaint, while the employer merely has to properly investigate and process the problem without necessarily resolving it. However, these procedures also create a convenient opportunity for the employer to internally refer it out to a non-confrontational and non-threatening process and attempt to resolve the problem before it becomes an entrenched conflict. This applies not only to issues of DDP/GPs but also to requests for flexible working and employment relations in general.

Experience tells us that in many employment cases the initial remedy is, more often than not, an apology. Accidents or mistakes usually occur as a result of ignorance, poor communication or genuine misunderstanding rather than malicious intent.

Strengths and Weaknesses of the In-house Mediation Approach

The strength of the in-house mediation approach is that it is cost effective for the employer because, for a minimal expense of management time, it can possibly avert the higher costs of a legal challenge. Even if a company is successful in defending a claim before a tribunal, it is unlikely to recover its legal spend.

The other major advantage of this approach is one of timing or what we call the "ripeness" of a dispute. By resolving the problem at a stage where rational thought is still roughly in proportion to emotive feelings, rather than just investigating it, there is greater likelihood that the reputations of both parties can be preserved and disruption to the overall operation of the company is kept to a minimum. As in eating fruit, if one judges properly, there is an optimum time for taking that first bite (see *Example 1*).

When is a Dispute "Ripe" for In-house Mediation?

- Where an apology or explanation will suffice.
- When a reputation can be preserved.
- Where alternative forms of compensation are available.
- Where a modification of existing policy can be negotiated.
- Where there is an acceptance of the likelihood of liability on the part of the company but a disagreement on the amount of financial compensation.
- Before lawyers are involved.

On a broader HR policy level, offering in-house mediation to employees shows that management is willing to go that extra mile to be reasonable and consider extraordinary circumstances that might have led to the problem in the first place. If the matter cannot be settled and ends up before an employment tribunal, the employer can use the fact of in-house mediation as evidence of how it acted fairly and reasonably. If management is indeed at fault, it offers them the opportunity to take corrective action, such as changing policy or properly defining it without suffering a loss of prestige or authority.

Sometimes managers have to make hard staffing decisions, especially in difficult economic times or in a merger situation, which may result in claims for unfair dismissal, constructive dismissal, or sex, race or disability discrimination (see Chapter 3 for a discussion of discrimination on the grounds of sexuality, religion and belief). In house mediation offers the management a "kite flying" opportunity to explain its side of the case and the reasons for its decisions while at the same time testing out pro-active offers such as outplacement, counselling and job recommendations, which may ease the pain for the employee.

Even with these benefits in mind, however, employees might resist the offer of in-house mediation as they may feel that even though the mediator is not their line manager, his or her loyalty lies with the management of the firm. The employee may also feel that while the process is conducted with the promise of confidentiality, in practice, bonding behind closed doors within the upper echelon of the company might preclude this. What some might term the "executive washroom key syndrome".

This hesitation by employees can only be overcome by building trust through experience and ensuring that those chosen to be conciliators have a strong reputation for integrity. Although in this model the company chose the conciliator, if doubts arise in the employee's mind at any time during the process, the company must be willing to offer a substitute (see *Example* 2). In practice, it means the company must train several of its managers or board members simultaneously in mediation and interpersonal skills or have access to multiple consultant mediators in order to practice this process effectively. This is especially true for SMEs with a flat management structure.

Example 1

Overview: A female sales executive returns from maternity leave to find her job altered. She faces rudeness and sexist comments from her male colleagues and then a few months later is made redundant. She plans to sue the firm for sexual discrimination and unfair dismissal, but agrees to in-house mediation before lodging a formal complaint with the employment tribunal. The in-house mediation by one of the firm's non-executive directors results in a solution agreed by both parties: a transfer for the woman to a sister company and no compensation other than a modest ex-gratia payment and relocation expenses in addition to her redundancy pay.

The Story: Sheena Toogood, aged 34, was a sales executive with Grunt Limited, an engineering company based in East Anglia. She had been with the company for four years and was the only female in the team with the exception of office administrative staff. She was quite good at her job and her performance ratings showed this, although after she became pregnant she began missing her sales targets. She took maternity leave and returned to find that the company had altered her job description (she was now called an account executive) as well as her sales territory. Instead of it being Suffolk, where she lived, she now had to work in Norfolk. As well as longer travel time, the hit ratio for closing sales was worse in that county and her prospects of achieving her targets were not so good as before she went on maternity leave.

(*continued*)

One morning, her colleague Bob Incorrect leers at her and says, "Well, a woman's place is in the home, *isn't it*?" The next day, Jim Loosetongue, another co-worker on the sales team mutters in her presence, "I suppose you will be wanting to go part time now with having to look after the babe." Sometime later on a business trip to Manchester, the male members of the sales team end up with a client at the Blue Danube night club, a lap dance parlour, while Sheena is left behind at her hotel, disappointed that she wasn't asked to join in.

She braves the comments of her colleagues and the pressure from her line manager because of low sales in her territory. But when she is selected for redundancy she loses patience. She considers that her selection was due to her pregnancy, made worse by the territory shift and not helped by the semi-hostile attitude of colleagues who usually share leads and co-operate.

During the period of redundancy consultation the company cannot find any alternative jobs despite a trawl nationally of the internal jobs database. They have nothing to offer her. She puts forward a grievance about the sexist remarks and awaits the final termination letter with some bitterness.

Bill Sensible is the regional managing director. He has been looking at the website of a progressive Bristol legal firm with ADR experience and sees that they can advise on in-house mediation. This attracts him.

The problems Sensible faces are as follows:

- Sheena is the lowest performer in her team.
- There is a need for redundancy.
- Because her line manager Dave Gruff has failed to handle the situation there is outright dislike amongst the sales team.
- Gruff has indicated he will leave if she is not selected to go and Gruff is good at sales, if not with people.
- Sensible concludes that Sheena has to go.

(continued)

On the other hand:

- He still quite likes Sheena and feels sorry for her.
- The year before his company lost a tribunal case on sex discrimination and he fears a repeat.
- There are some arguments that her performance has been affected a) by her pregnancy and b) by the company's action in reorganising the region (although this was imposed by head office in France and was not generated by any motive of causing detriment to her).
- Gruff will make a bad witness and he has mishandled the situation.

Rather than allow the conflict to pass into an over-ripe and aggressive stage, he decides to bring in Oliver Smooth, a locally based non-executive director of Grunt Limited. Oliver is a recently retired City commercial lawyer. Sensible thinks Smooth may have just the touch needed to solve this problem without too much expense and without a high profile fight.

Sheena looks at the situation like this. On the one hand:

- She is angry and hurt.
- She has been treated badly and when Gruff was told about the upsetting comments, he said "Don't be silly".
- If she had been given another four months, pipeline orders would have increased her sales figures dramatically.
- The redundancy is not fair when Joe Sloppy is staying on with similar figures to hers.

On the other hand:

- She has not got legal expense insurance or enough money to fight a case privately.
- Her lawyer will do a "no win no fee" but wants a cost uplift that will mean her net recovery (if she wins) is likely to be less than she needs to provide for her family during the anticipated unemployment period.
- She left her grievance rather late.
- She likes working in sales and thinks it unlikely there will be another opportunity for her if she leaves Grunt Limited.

(*continued*)

Sheena receives a telephone call from Oliver Smooth. He tells her that the company would like to see if things could be sorted out amicably without a tribunal application. He tells her frankly that he is a director of Grunt and this cannot be overlooked but he assures her that he will treat her comments in confidence and offers to confirm this in writing. He wants to look at the problem sensibly and without hostility. He apologises for the fact that she was so upset by remarks from fellow employees and gets their conversation off to a good start. They agree to meet at the company premises the next day.

When they meet again Smooth reminds her that this internal mediation is informal, confidential and either side can break off at any time. If it looks like there is a way to resolve this situation, then he will talk to Gruff and Sensible for final agreement. He will do all the talking to the company for the time being. Sheena agrees but says she is a bit concerned because her solicitor, James Aggressive, has advised her that she might be conceding her strong legal position by talking to the company in this way. Smooth gets her agreement for him to discuss matters with Aggressive.

This he does and manages to gain acceptance from the lawyer for mediation to take place (otherwise, thinks Aggressive, Sheena might run the risk of being penalised for not taking settlement as far as she might). It is a condition imposed by Aggressive that this discussion is "without prejudice" (cannot be referred to in the tribunal) and takes no longer than three days since the relevant time for the first sex discrimination comments runs out in five days and a claim has to be issued by then to avoid part of Sheena's case failing.

Over several cups of coffee Smooth lets Sheena tell her story. Perceptibly she relaxes as she sees that he is not trying to get an advantage and is genuinely listening sympathetically. It becomes clear that she likes working and is not keen to go onto state benefits to look after the child her mother cares for in the day. She also likes sales. It is also clear that Sheena too recognises that relationships in the team are so bad it is unlikely her continued employment with Grunt can work. An idea strikes Smooth and he asks Sheena if she would mind meeting him again the following afternoon. She agrees.

(*continued*)

Smooth is non-executive director of another sister company, Bulk Limited, operating from Felixstowe. It deals in freight transport both in the UK and abroad. It has a sales team and he thinks there is a vacancy. There is nothing suitable in the East of England within Grunt — that has already been checked out. He calls the managing director of Bulk who is happy for the matter to be progressed, though insists on an interview.

Smooth calls Sheena and drives her over to Bulk where she makes a good impression. The salary for the job is lower but there are good commission incentives for successful sales operatives. Sheena quite likes the set up and working back in Suffolk would be helpful.

She calls Aggressive who reminds her that she could be entitled to £10,000 plus for injury to feelings and another £10,000 for redundancy/compensation for unfair dismissal. He does admit though that he has not run up a large bill so far, only about £400. She sits down again with Smooth and lets him know her thoughts. He tells her that the Felixstowe job is hers if she wants it. She lets him know she is in debt to her lawyer and that the new job is on a lower salary. He knows what she is talking about and has already spoken to Sensible. Her notice pay can be added to an ex gratia payment and made free of tax if Grunt has breached the contract and is paying damages as she has no PILON clause in her contract (pay in lieu of notice that makes notice pay taxable). They think notice plus £1500 is acceptable, but even £2000 is a good deal.

Sheena is told there will be a lump sum of £1500 on top of her notice if she takes the job and signs a compromise agreement — more money for Aggressive. She reckons it will take four months to equalise income with her present job. That will set her back £250 per month. The balance will pay Aggressive and give her some loose change. She tries to get a bit more. Smooth tells her that she can have another £250 and she agrees.

Later a compromise agreement is signed at the same time as Bulk's job offer is accepted. Sheena leaves with a big bunch of flowers from Sensible, Smooth and the office girls. Gruff and his crew retire to the Black Lion, another dirty day's work done.

(*continued*)

Grunt has saved a lot of money and some face. It is likely that even if Sheena had not won at tribunal this story would have hit the local press. Sheena has got another job and one she thinks she will like. Smooth has justified his high pay (he was one of the first to seek a rise after the Higgs Report). Sensible can keep relying on Gruff's uncanny sales ability. Gruff can keep on treating people badly. Aggressive doesn't earn a big fee, but he did get £250 for the compromise agreement. The local employment tribunal has space for another case.

Example 2

Overview: The general manager of a car dealership is sacked under pressure from the manufacturer after his managing director gives false information about him. In-house mediation is attempted, but no deal is achieved.

The Story: Joe Dapper is the general manager of Fourbyfour Limited, a dealership for a Japanese manufacturer in the West of England selling larger cars and trucks. The manufacturer has a programme of modernising their dealerships and making them more efficient financially and the Fourbyfour dealership is one of those chosen.

David Crump founded the company and there are a number of the Crump family still inhabiting the business, especially John Crump, the finance director, Peter Crump, who works in Kuwait and David's son, Alan Crump, who is the managing director. Alan is gay and complaints have been made by the staff about gay pornography invading the company computer network as a result of nocturnal web surfing by Alan. He is able and has taken the company a long way since his father's day. Alan is, however, unscrupulous and ruthless.

Dapper is organised and very loyal to the Crump family. He will never set the world alight, but has managed the salesmen and mechanics well over the five years since he was promoted from the sales team leader to become general manager. He keeps careful records. He reports to Alan.

(*continued*)

It was agreed 18 months ago that Alan would develop the dealership in East Devon, a new territory given to them by the Japanese when the previous dealership there went bankrupt. Dapper is directly responsible for sales targets in the three other divisions of Fourbyfour Limited. The reason Alan wanted East Devon is that he likes hunting and has joined a prestigious hunt in that area. He contends that mixing with the moneyed classes in the richest part of Devon will open doors for the business.

Yutaka Oyota from the Japanese manufacturer orders an undercover inspection visit to Fourbyfour Limited and finds that there is no one at the main showroom to demonstrate a new vehicle. The Japanese are alerted to a possible problem dealer. They raise the issue with Alan at the next worldwide meeting of dealerships in the Caribbean and say, in addition, that sales in East Devon are not sufficient. Alan blames Dapper and puts it down to the fact that Dapper has just had a birth in his family and has taken time off to be with his wife, which he is perfectly entitled to. He doesn't say any of this to Dapper.

Sales in East Devon continue to flag and the Japanese raise the issue again saying that the only way Fourbyfour Limited can keep East Devon is if Dapper is replaced. Alan is now alarmed, but he keeps his head and manages to remove all the files relating to his responsibility for that area. He takes advice from Denzil Dare, the bright new employment lawyer at Dewey Cheatem & Howe, the company lawyers. Dare tells him that in certain circumstances pressure from significant outsiders such as the Japanese can amount to "some other substantial reason" (SOSR). To use this as a ground for dismissal will obviate the need to go through warnings, training and the whole process of making a dismissal fair in cases of poor performance. He elects to go down that route to hold off the pressure from the manufacturer.

Dare advises him that the new DDP/GPs will require a letter to be sent to Dapper telling him what is envisaged and why and giving him the opportunity to respond at a meeting to be convened shortly. The letter is sent off and the next day Dapper telephones in a state of mixed upset and anger. He rejects the assertion that he has been the cause of the problem in East Devon and says he wants to argue against his dismissal. He contends that on the day of the mystery visit, Alan was on duty.

(*continued*)

Alan had heard about in-house mediation from Dare. He hopes this matter can be comfortably swept under the carpet and decides to ask his father, David Crump, to step into the role of mediator. David is 76 years old and retired, but still takes an interest in Fourbyfour Limited and above all is respected and admired by Dapper. Alan believes he is being rather clever.

Dapper agrees to take part as long as he still has the right to attend a meeting with Alan if mediation does not work. This is confirmed to him. He then meets David and tells him that it was Alan and not him who was responsible for East Devon. David listens carefully, but then asks to see the board minutes for the time when the addition to the dealership occurred. Unfortunately these are missing. "So it boils down to his word against yours then?" he asks. "I suppose so," says Dapper sadly, "but have you asked Yutaka Oyota if he will change his mind?" David nods and says he has tried, but that they are adamant. He goes on to say Fourbyfour Limited intend bringing back Peter Crump from Kuwait to be general manager and that the only option is to put Dapper back as head of sales, but this would mean a cut in salary.

By this time Dapper is upset and asks to leave. He feels he can no longer work out his notice. He calls a friend who refers him to Fred Fox of Kennels, a firm specialising in employment law and mediation. Fox tells him that the issue is not black and white, but that the mileage claims put in by Alan for his Porsche could tip the balance as they show regular trips to East Devon and the odd night at the Suckling Sow, a favourite haunt of his in the area. The claim could be enhanced by a victimisation claim since Dapper complained to John Crump, the financial director, about the pornography — the downloading was a breach of the written contractual policy on e-mail and the Internet. The pressure on Dapper regarding East Devon started almost immediately after that. This is a claim under the **Public Interest Disclosure Act 1998** (Whistleblowing) for which damages can be awarded. There is other evidence of Alan being vindictive. Overall, with six months' notice, a basic and compensatory award and a bit for victimisation, the claim could top £40,000.

(*continued*)

Dapper had not mentioned Alan's downloading of pornography to David out of respect for the old man's feelings. He was aware that David had no idea that his son was gay. He does not want to accept demotion and anyway, his loathing of Alan is only surpassed by his dislike of Peter. He decides he must leave and pursue a claim for compensation, but through the law. He cannot face bargaining with David. He is still saddened to have to do this to a family whose other members he has always had excellent relations with. He approaches a big dealership in Exeter who tell him that they would be delighted to take him on as general manager as soon as he is free.

The formality of the meeting with Alan takes place and Dapper is dismissed. The appeal put in on the advice of Fox (otherwise the employee can't apply to the employment tribunal) is turned down and an application is prepared to lodge at the Exeter Tribunal. Fox mentions to Dare over the telephone that it contains the victimisation allegation. Alan is now terrified that the allegation of his spreading pornography through the company computer will come out during the hearing. He begs Dare to speak nicely to Fox in an attempt to mediate this case confidentially using an external mediator.

In Example 2, the in-house mediator, David, was too close to one of the parties, his son Alan, to be impartial or objective, especially in the face of an unsubstantiated charge. It was also clearly not in David's family's interest to challenge their Japanese masters, so there was little scope for creative problem-solving, such as we saw in Example 1. Furthermore, Dapper was put in the invidious position of having to choose between seriously embarrassing David, a man he truly respected, by giving him information about his son Alan, or walk away from his job. He never really had a chance to speak confidentially with the mediator. The first lesson here is that choosing the right person to be the mediator at the outset is crucial to the success of the process. The second is that the mediator cannot just be an agent for the employer. He or she must equally be there for the employee.

External Mediation

Despite the best efforts of a progressive management, there will be times when the in-house mediation procedure will fail and that under the three-step DDP/GP guidelines the employer has to notify the employee of its decision and then offer the employee one final time to appeal that decision before he or she may proceed with his or her application to the employment tribunal.

While the law has been designed to allow the parties yet another chance to defuse the conflict and stand back from the abyss of antagonism, experience in multi-step procedures leads to the belief that most parties will squander this opportunity and use it as a necessary formality to proceed to the employment tribunal.

It is at this point that the calculus of the conflict changes. Whereas steps one and two of the DDP/GP procedure are more driven from the employer's perspective by the need to define the problem and maintain control of the situation, after step three, the key components of the equation become the cost implications of settling what has now turned into an emotionally charged and possibly vindictive conflict, and the risks of losing altogether before the tribunal and having a penalty imposed. Obviously, the higher value the claim, the greater the risk.

Yet even after step three has been taken, and even up to the time of the tribunal hearing itself, there is another way to tackle this brinkmanship. It is time to call in the external mediator (*Example 3*).

Unlike the in-house mediator, the external mediator is an independent. He or she has no ties whatsoever with either party. The process itself often addresses the inherent power imbalance between employee and employer, because both parties have to agree on the selection of the mediator and share in the cost of the process, which, in itself, takes place at a neutral venue. But perhaps most important of all, the power imbalance is addressed in two specific ways. The first is that the employee can bring along legal representation, who as a professional negotiator is probably in a stronger position and is perhaps more capable of presenting the client's position and assessing the legal strength of the employer's position. Secondly, the mediator, being neutral, is able to "reality check" the employer's defences with hard, probing questions that the employee could probably not get away with during the in-house mediation.

How External Mediation Works

- Talks are held privately at a neutral venue.
- The mediator is an independent person who has no ties to either the employer or employee.
- Both parties agree to the choice of the mediator.
- Parties are allowed to bring legal representatives.

- The mediator initially meets both sides jointly and may then decide to meet the parties separately.
- Confidentiality is guaranteed.
- Statements made or evidence given during the mediation cannot later be used at a tribunal.
- The mediator reports back to both parties.
- If the case is not settled, the case can still proceed to the tribunal.
- Costs are shared (but a settlement can lead to the employer agreeing to foot the bill).

The cost implications of dispute resolution are paramount to every manager. By this stage, the employer has engaged the legal services of a solicitor and possibly a barrister. It has to factor in that a large part of its legal spend will come at the beginning of the process as its legal team prepares the case for tribunal. It must weigh the added cost implications of engaging in the mediation process against the risk of a further legal spend at the tribunal hearing and the possibility that a tribunal award will exceed the price extracted from a negotiated settlement. More importantly, perhaps, the employer must weigh up the relative costs of engaging in the ongoing bi-lateral negotiation process between solicitors or the one off opportunity of a multilateral negotiation using an intermediary external mediator.

When is an Employment Dispute not "Ripe" for Mediation?

- When the employer wants to set a precedent for defending plans or policies.
- When the employee is determined to "make an example" of the company.

Over 10 years of commercial mediation experience in this country has clearly defined what parties like and don't like about the mediation process. What parties like about mediation can be summed up as follows:

- It is "interest-based" rather than "rights-based". Parties are able to look for an outcome that may meet a variety of needs beyond just what they are entitled to under the law.
- During mediation a range of settlement options can be discussed, including ones that are not within the power of an employment tribunal, such as agreeing the terms of a reference.

- The discussions are non-binding. You can suggest ideas without being committed to them until you have reached a final agreement.
- You can walk away from the table at any time and you haven't forfeited any of your legal options.
- Mediation is commonly directed towards the creation of relevant norms rather than conformity to those supported by the formal legal system.
- It can be a cathartic experience. It offers an opportunity to state a case without constraint.
- Both the process itself and atmosphere at the talks are informal.
- There are no legal technicalities or rules of evidence.
- Mediation allows for a variety of stakeholders in a dispute to come to the negotiation table.
- Correctly used, mediation is a pro-active approach to information-sharing about risks, benefits, and operational and emotional issues.
- Pro-active mediation can introduce external expertise for such things as fact-finding, independent audits and verification, and neutral expert guidance.
- Lawyers like mediation because it gives them an off-the-record chance to assess the strengths of their respective cases.
- Claimants and applicants like mediation because it gives them a chance to participate in the settlement process.
- Defendants and respondents like mediation because they feel that the mediator provides a window to the applicant's way of thinking.

To be fair, there are those who are not enthusiastic about mediation or conciliation because they cannot see what it adds to the normal negotiation process, or that it may indicate to the other side that they have a weak case because they are willing to compromise. There are employers who want to avoid, delay or minimise any payment they might have to make and rely on the tactic that the time and money it takes to get to the tribunal will make the employee abandon the case.

On the other hand, there are employees who are sceptical about the mediation process and who want their day in court. They want justice not compromise and believe they will win.

Most of these emotions are driven by the fear that mediation undermines the validity of their argument and the legitimacy of their claim. Nothing could be further from the truth.

The role of the mediator is not to sit in judgment and make rulings or awards about claims, but to facilitate an exchange of views and, hopefully, establish a dialogue between parties in a dispute so they can reach a settlement that they can live with. No one really wins in employment litigation. Legal costs are rarely recoverable, hard-earned reputations are damaged, and future prospects for employment are clouded because an employee who has sued an employer may well carry the stigma with him or her.

The mediator starts from the premise that all parties are legitimately at the negotiation table and that all aspects of their argument are entitled to be heard. Their role is to guarantee "air time" so that parties feel that they have had a chance to present their points of view. A mediator is there to make sure that neither side is pressured into settlement. Perhaps more importantly, he or she is there to make sure parties fully understand the terms and implications of any proposed settlement, because once a settlement is signed, it becomes as binding as any other contract in the eyes of the law.

Both employers and employees can take comfort in the knowledge that if mediation proves unsuccessful, and the case goes before the tribunal, the mediator cannot be called as a witness as he or she is a signatory to the confidentiality agreement, which prohibits any information learned during the mediation process from being used as evidence for a tribunal.

What General Qualities Should you Look for in a Mediator?

In the mediation model we have been describing, anyone can be an in-house mediator subject to training in interpersonal and communication skills and mediation techniques. There are no pre-requisites in terms of professional or educational qualifications. Consultant mediators or external neutral mediators through independent providers have already undergone the necessary training and accreditation and their credentials should be easy to verify, provided you go through a recognised ADR provider.

Mediators have to adapt to different parties and different situations. More importantly, they are agents to all parties. In our in-house mediation model, we have suggested that companies can use managers, non-executive board members or take on consultant mediators. But this is by no means limited to these categories. For example, you may want to call upon a retired former employee whose loyalty and knowledge of the firm you value.

No two mediators will ever have the same style or approach, as every person's perception of the elements of conflict differs. What we can suggest from our experience is that the more successful mediators usually demonstrate the qualities of credibility, humility, intellectual rigour, integrity, patience, persistence and energy. The last quality is extremely important, because mediation can be a very intense and emotional process that requires a great deal of concentration and stamina.

Both the employer and employee will be looking to the mediator to take a pro-active role and, through active listening to all the interests and positions of the parties, to come up with suggestions for creatively crafting ways to break deadlocks and facilitate settlements. But remember that the mediator is not there to be a judge and decide who wins.

Example 3

Overview: Follow-on of the case of the dealership employee who is sacked under pressure from the manufacturer after his managing director gives false information about him. In-house mediation is attempted, but no deal is achieved. The dispute is referred to external mediation after an appeal is turned down under Step 3 of the DDP/GP.

The Story: Joe Dapper goes to see Fred Fox about his case. The internal conciliation has failed but he has two reasons for not wanting this to go all the way to an employment tribunal hearing. First, he is still grateful to the Crumps for having given him a career. Second, and more importantly now, he has a job and thus his claim will be reduced by the income he receives from his new employment, even though his start is delayed three months. It makes sense to try to cut a deal.

Fox sees this, but with an eye to his own billing and to make Fourbyfour Limited realise they have a fight on their hands, he thinks an application should be made to the employment tribunal. He wants the other side to see just how badly his client has been treated and what will come out at the hearing.

(*continued*)

Fox has been in touch with Denzil Dare who indicated that this is a genuine SOSR case and the Japanese really are insisting on Dapper's head. They are ready to defend. He does let slip that there may be value in an informal discussion. Fox notes this and feels reassured that a bit of toughness up front will not prevent a final deal. He doesn't appreciate that Dare is seriously offended by the rather brusque ignoring of his tentative feeler for settlement talks. He is determined to punish the older lawyer for his perceived arrogance — they will have a fight on their hands.

Dapper himself is quite shrewd and agrees that to go back cap in hand to Dare and renew the initiative for direct discussion will look like weakness. He agrees that proceedings should be issued. He now feels that he wants to be a direct part of the settlement process and having read the pamphlet on mediation in Kennels' reception, he insists that Fox write to Dare with a formal offer of mediation with an independent neutral. Mediation gives the lay client (here the employee) an opportunity to influence the outcome of the negotiations beyond merely assenting to a figure.

Dare sees this offer and, still angry with Fox, is not very impressed. He does pass it on to Fourbyfour Limited. Alan Crump reads it and is about to put it in the bin when David Crump asks him what it is about. By now David has seen that there are allegations of whistleblowing and victimisation arising out of the gay porn saga. He is very anxious that this does not seep out into the rather conservative Devon business community. Pretty angry by now, he insists that his son instruct Dare to respond positively to the offer of mediation.

There are squabbles about the choice of mediator and the venue. These are sorted out and the mediation is set to take place four weeks before the date issued for the tribunal hearing and therefore before major costs are incurred on witness statements and disclosure of documents.

The costs of contesting a case in the employment tribunal and of using a skilled mediator have to be looked at carefully and compared with the risks involved and the amounts at stake. Dapper's legal costs (in addition to his £40,000 claim) could mount up to between £7000-£10,000 by the end of the hearing. Even this amount could increase, because there is sometimes a second hearing to decide the amount of compensation to be paid.

(*continued*)

Mediation can cost between £1000-£2000 or more for a whole day, though most mediators will work on an hourly basis if the settlement time is less. This would normally be split equally between the parties. That is just the cost of the mediator. Each side has to add on its own lawyer costs.

The selected mediator, Sheila Dogood, is an employment lawyer who is an accredited mediator for the ADR Group in Bristol, a nationally recognised independent dispute resolution company. She talks to Fox and Dare before the session and ensures they are familiar with the process. She ensures that the Fourbyfour Limited representative, John Crump the finance director, is authorised to settle in the sort of range likely to be necessary to get a solution on the day. She warns that having to telephone head office for instructions causes a serious loss of momentum in the process — it can prevent a deal arising.

Everyone meets at rooms in the Institute of Directors building and as pre-agreed, no one has appointments later on that day that could mean a premature end to the session.

After a short opening meeting with all present at which presentations of each side's case are put to Sheila, she separates Dapper and his lawyer from the Crumps and their lawyer (David and Alan Crump have come along at the last minute) and the mediation starts in earnest.

Sheila has already seen case summary papers prepared by both sides and so has a fairly good idea of the basic facts and legal arguments. To get people relaxed and to trust her, she asks each lawyer in turn to let their client tell her what they think about the case and where they would like to be at the end of the day. She discovers that Dapper and the Crumps both want to settle, even though their lawyers have a very different view of the merits. She meets with each side, listening, but also playing devil's advocate and asking challenging questions. She asks Dapper why he is unable to produce any documentation proving Alan accepted the East Devon territory. She asks Alan if he accepts that there is a formal contractual e-mail and Internet policy on downloading pornography and that Dapper made a formal complaint to John Crump about this. "Did you download this material?" she asks, and he admits, hanging his head, that he did. There is an awkward family moment and she decides to leave the room and let the Crumps stew for a few minutes.

(*continued*)

Dapper admits to her that he has another job. She accepts that this is confidential information not to be passed on, but she uses it to lower his expectations of a big payout. "What do you really think a tribunal will award you in the event of a win?" He and Fox both accept that about £20,000 could be cut from their claim. "Give me a figure I can ask the other side for," she asks. Eventually they agree she can offer a reduction in the claim figure, but only if the other side make an offer first.

Back with the Crumps she can see the tension is still high and the family tell her they will not be blackmailed into paying a ridiculous figure. They will offer £12,000. She returns to Dapper and Fox who counter with an offer of £30,000 as well as a very good reference as a settlement.

After two hours of bargaining and a good look by both sides at what they stand to lose if the case goes to the employment tribunal, the deal struck is £22,000 and a good reference, each party picking up their costs.

This case was ripe for settlement, but once the lawyers fell out they were unable to do it directly. It was ripe because the costs of fighting it were too high in relation to the chances for either side of a satisfactory result from a fought hearing.

It was suitable for mediation, and in real life, settled in five hours. The mediator challenged and persuaded the parties, but never imposed any decision. The outcome was something that both parties could live with. In business, that's the bottom line.

Example 4

Overview: Case of a manager who cannot relate to an employee from another culture and background to her own.

The Story: Maggie Manager has a real problem with one of her staff, Ashley. He is a black man who was born and raised in Nigeria. She ignores his suggestions and comments and this gets him wound up. As a result he gets frustrated and angry and loses his temper. Maggie uses this against him and has questioned his conduct. Now Ashley doesn't even bother saying anything in meetings, as it is easier not to do so. Maggie has now questioned his commitment to the project they are working on. Ashley was already angry and responded that he is not committed to the project.

(*continued*)

Maggie wants to sack Ashley for not having commitment. Ashley is unhappy at work and is thinking of leaving. Maggie starts formal disciplinary proceedings against Ashley. In return he raises a grievance against her because of the way she has treated him. He says that it may be racially motivated as she is picking on him and not others.

The managing director hears of this and calls in Samantha Senior, the financial director, who has had in-house mediation training. Samantha meets with Maggie privately. Maggie tells Samantha that there is no racial motive to her treatment, but she accepts that she has got frustrated at Ashley's lack of commitment and the final straw was when he said himself that he is not committed to the project. She says that Ashley has always been a good worker.

Samantha then meets with Ashley. She allows Ashley the opportunity to tell her all about the treatment he has had from Maggie. He is clearly upset by it and Samantha lets him get it off his chest. He says that he has always been happy working there and thought there was a future for him in the company. Now he is not so sure. Samantha asks him about his commitment to the project. Ashley says that he is not committed to it. Samantha pauses and thinks. Then she asks, "What do you mean by commitment?" Ashley explains that, to him, *commitment* is what you give your wife and children, not your job. He says that he is dedicated to his job. In the culture he grew up in, there is a difference in the meaning of the two words.

Samantha gets Ashley's consent to tell Maggie about this. When she tells her, Maggie realises that there has been a communication problem and a misunderstanding. She accepts that she should involve Ashley more in discussions. Ashley is happy with this. The project was completed ahead of schedule and the clients were so pleased with the result that three more projects have come in, with one proviso: that Maggie and Ashley are the team that work on the projects.

Example 5

Overview: Case of an employee whose request for flexible working hours so that he can look after his child is hastily denied by his manager.

(*continued*)

The Story: John Secretary is a male secretary. His employers, Delta Drinks, are proud that they are a progressive firm who are not afraid to break traditional stereotypes about secretaries only being female. In fact, local newspapers have written about Delta and John and how forward-thinking Delta are. John hopes the role is a stepping-stone to management responsibilities.

John is a father of a three-year-old boy. He wants to be able to work part time for two days a week and full time for the other three days to help with caring for the child. He makes a formal request for flexible working to his manager, Chris Nocompromise. He knows that Delta are very willing to be flexible as in the last six months alone, five women have been allowed to alter their working hours to fit in with their childcare arrangements.

Chris takes one look at the request and immediately says, "No way". He says that John cannot have time off as he is a man and men don't do this. He then makes a snide remark about John being a secretary. John is very upset by this and takes legal advice. He is told that Chris's comments would enable John to resign and claim constructive unfair dismissal. He would also have a claim for sex discrimination and a failure by Delta to provide a considered response to the request for flexible working.

John would like to stay at Delta as he can see himself progressing up the ladder. However, he is livid at the way he has been treated and wants to sue them. His lawyer has just read a good book about resolving work place disputes by using in-house mediation. He notes that Delta has a policy covering this. He persuades Chris to use the in-house mediation procedure offered by the company.

The mediator is the business development manager, Martin Middle, who is well respected within the company. He meets John and Chris separately and lets them tell him what has happened. He then asks each of them what they want. Chris says that he wants a full-time secretary as his workload often means urgent letters must be typed and sent straight away. He also admits that he can tell John is very able and he doesn't want John taking a better job and leaving him in the lurch, so he sees this as a way of testing John's loyalty. Finally he says that they would be better off without John anyway as he must be "a poof". Chris raises his eyebrow, nudges Martin and laughs a dirty laugh.

(*continued*)

Martin thinks that this is very inappropriate. He asks Chris whether he thinks comments like that help the situation. Chris realises that they do not and says so. He also says that John gets comments like this from some of the female secretaries, but it is really because they are jealous that he is very able. Chris admits that John could do much higher-level work.

Martin asks John what he wants. John says that he would like to stay, but wants compensation and talks about thousands of pounds. Martin asks John how realistic this is. John thinks for a while and admits that the figures are based on press articles. Martin then asks what John really wants. John says that he really wants to stay and to be allowed more flexible working hours. He also says that he hopes he can move on to management level soon. He says that if this were likely, the compensation would not be an issue, as he would get a better salary anyway. Martin asks John whether he can disclose this to Chris. John is reluctant as he thinks it puts him in a worse position. Martin says that it is up to John, but he thinks it would help if he could disclose it. John agrees.

Martin tells Chris what John has just said. Chris thinks about it. He says that John is very good at what he does. He also says that there is a vacant trainee manager's role at the moment. Martin says that he knows Sarah, who is a part-time secretary, wants to extend her hours. Chris suggests that maybe John could be promoted to trainee manager, a role that could accommodate the flexible working request, and Sarah could become his full-time secretary. Martin suggests this to John. He accepts.

The matter is resolved amicably, with minimal disruption to the business. In fact, the outcome means that Delta Drinks are making best use of their resources and therefore making more money. There is still a slight atmosphere between John and Chris, but the matter was resolved in a way that neither was right or wrong and therefore, neither lost face.

Costs Analysis

The curve below is usual. That is, after an initial communication between employer and lawyer, costs start to rise steeply as the facts are gone into and a response (form IT3) is filed. Costs rise a bit more slowly thereafter while statements are obtained and other preparation is undergone. But then things heat up with the exchange of witness statements and a flurry of activity leading to the hearing.

Chart 5 — Legal costs for a contentious tribunal case

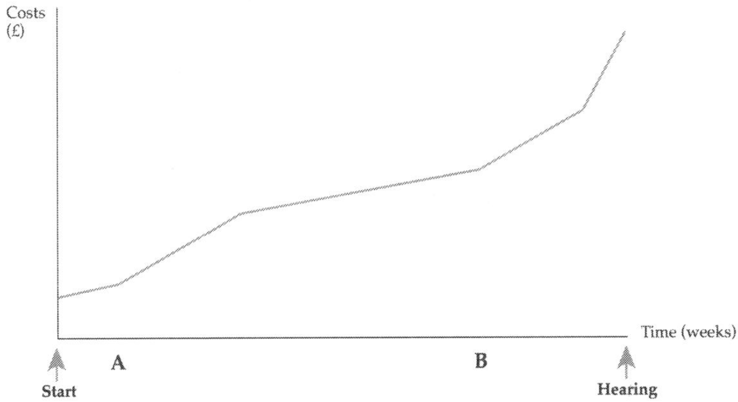

The cost of external mediation is likely to be equivalent to the cost of a day at tribunal, with the addition of half of the mediator's cost (say £750). Common sense, from a cost perspective, suggests attempting mediation (if it is otherwise suitable) either at point A (before heavy legal costs are expended) or at point B (before the costs of pre-hearing activity). In the case of Fourbyfour and Dapper, the mediation would have cost the employer £1000 for lawyers' fees and £750 for the mediation plus VAT. However, a two-day hearing might well have cost (including all legal costs before hearing) £7000 to £9000. Mediation at point A is clearly advantageous financially. At point B there is much more information and this may itself tend to generate settlement moves. There is no clear-cut answer to when, but as costs get higher they themselves become the reason for continuing the fight. On the whole, it makes sense to try mediation early.

CHAPTER 6

Employment Contracts: Getting It Right From The Start

The contract of employment and associated documentation, such as policies and procedures, are fundamental to the employment relationship. They define what duties the employer and the employee owe to each other and in any dispute they provide the first point of reference to see what the parties agreed.

We have seen many employers who think that as there is no contract in place the employee is in a weak position. In actual fact, experience suggests that the opposite is true: those employers without proper contractual documentation in place usually end up in a worse position. The reason is that without a definitive piece of paper saying what the employer can or cannot do, an argument will invariably ensue and then it is up to the employment tribunal or court to decide the matter. This means that the employer will incur the time, cost and hassle of going to the tribunal and then may lose the case. If a contract is clear and covers the relevant points, the matter will be resolved at an early stage.

Therefore, having clear and well-drafted contractual documentation in place is the first and simplest way of resolving disputes internally and quickly.

Example 1

Amy goes to her employer, Beta Brothers Greengrocers, and asks for a week's holiday starting in two days' time. She has no contract of employment as her boss, Simon Slack, keeps saying he'll get round to it next week. Amy apologises for it being a last minute request, but she has just decided on the spur of the moment to go. Beta Brothers are approaching their financial year end and it's the busiest time of the year for them. They cannot afford for Amy to go away for a week, as she is needed to help with the year end work. They say no. Amy is really angry as her colleague Bill was allowed to take two weeks off with little notice when he won a holiday for two in a local prize vegetable competition a few months ago. She is cross and accuses Beta Brothers of unfair behaviour and sex discrimination and she threatens to resign and sue them for constructive unfair dismissal as well.

The above shows how quickly a dispute escalates. Beta Brothers now have an angry staff member threatening to sue them. This will cost Beta Brothers management time to investigate and try and resolve it; it will also affect the staff morale at the most important time in the year. Added to this, Beta Brothers' managers will have sleepless nights worrying about what might happen if Amy leaves (she is the only one who knows certain information needed for the year end process). What if they are sued? Beta Brothers may end up losing Amy if she decides to look for a job elsewhere. Amy may just go on holiday anyway, calling in sick, and this will lead to a difficult issue for Beta Brothers to deal with.

This issue could have been dealt with quickly, easily and with little or no disruption to the employment relationship between Amy and Beta Brothers. More importantly, the overall efficiency and cohesion of the business would not have been affected at such a key time.

(continued)

The simple solution would have been a contract of employment with clear rules about holidays. The contract could lay down a minimum period of notice for taking holidays, for example at least as much notice as number of days holiday requested. In addition would be a provision stating that holiday could only be taken during year end in exceptional circumstances and at management's absolute discretion. Amy would have known this and probably not even thought about taking the holiday at that time. Even if she asked, Slack could have referred to the contract when turning down her request to show that he was acting in accordance with the contract and not treating her any differently to other staff.

The above highlights how a contract can avoid disputes arising. This will not always be the case, but it certainly is a useful tool in managing conflicts in the workplace. The contract also provides a valuable way of reinforcing disciplinary matters. For example, if a member of staff is misusing his or her computer and downloading pornographic pictures from the Internet. This is clearly inappropriate behaviour and if you dismiss him or her for gross misconduct with no notice, that's OK isn't it? Unfortunately, you may not be completely safe. An employment tribunal looking at whether the dismissal was fair or unfair will consider, amongst other things, whether the employee had been told not to do this and whether he or she was aware of the serious manner in which his or her conduct would be treated. In the absence of an Internet policy setting out what is and is not acceptable use there would probably not be a finding of unfair dismissal.

This might seem very harsh, but it can easily be overcome by setting out an e-mail and Internet policy, making it clear that accessing or downloading pornographic images is not allowed and will be treated very seriously and may lead to instant dismissal without notice.

The importance of the contract and policies and procedures is plain. They help to avoid disputes and allow management to tell staff what sort of behaviour is unacceptable.

However, because of its important nature, it is vital that the paperwork is right for your business. Contracts should be tailored to fit your business. Section 1 of the **Employment Rights Act 1996** sets out compulsory details that must be given to all employees within two months of their start date.

Section 1 Employment Rights Act 1996

(1) Where an employee begins employment with an employer, the employer shall give to the employee a written statement of particulars of employment.

(2) The statement may (subject to section 2(4)) be given in instalments and (whether or not given in instalments) shall be given not later than two months after the beginning of the employment.

(3) The statement shall contain particulars of:

- (a) the names of the employer and employee
- (b) the date when the employment began, and
- (c) the date on which the employee's period of continuous employment began (taking into account any employment with a previous employer that counts towards that period).

(4) The statement shall also contain particulars, as at a specified date not more than seven days before the statement (or the instalment containing them) is given, of:

- (a) the scale or rate of remuneration or the method of calculating remuneration
- (b) the intervals at which remuneration is paid (that is, weekly, monthly or other specified intervals)
- (c) any terms and conditions relating to hours of work (including any terms and conditions relating to normal working hours)
- (d) any terms and conditions relating to any of the following:
  - (i) entitlement to holidays, including public holidays, and holiday pay (the particulars given being sufficient to enable the employee's entitlement, including any entitlement to accrued holiday pay on the termination of employment, to be precisely calculated)
  - (ii) incapacity for work due to sickness or injury, including any provision for sick pay, and
  - (iii) pensions and pension schemes

(*continued*)

(e) the length of notice that the employee is obliged to give and entitled to receive to terminate his or her contract of employment

(f) the title of the job that the employee is employed to do or a brief description of the work for which he or she is employed

(g) where the employment is not intended to be permanent, the period for which it is expected to continue or, if it is for a fixed term, the date when it is to end

(h) either the place of work or, where the employee is required or permitted to work at various places, an indication of that and of the address of the employer

(i) any collective agreements which directly affect the terms and conditions of the employment including, where the employer is not a party, the persons by whom they were made, and

(j) where the employee is required to work outside the United Kingdom for a period of more than one month:
   (i) the period for which he or she is to work outside the United Kingdom
   (ii) the currency in which remuneration is to be paid while he or she is working outside the United Kingdom
   (iii) any additional remuneration payable to him or her, and any benefits to be provided to or in respect of him or her, by reason of his or her being required to work outside the United Kingdom, and
   (iv) any terms and conditions relating to his or her return to the United Kingdom.

Chapter 2 deals with the three-step statutory Disciplinary and Dismissal Procedure (DDP) and the three-step Grievance Procedure (GP). Once this is in force (in October 2004), the Statement of Terms and Conditions must also contain details of these procedures.

If an employee is successful in a claim before the employment tribunal for, amongst other things, unfair dismissal or sex, race or disability discrimination, then additional compensation of between two and four weeks' pay (based on the statutory limit for a week's pay) will be awarded if a proper statement of terms has not been given.

As well as the contract, it is sensible to have a staff handbook, which lays down policies and procedures. These do not normally form part of the contract of employment, but are guidelines for how the employer will treat certain situations. As an employer, you should follow these guidelines, but if you do not then this will not be a breach of contract, although it may well indicate an unfair dismissal. By not making the policies contractual, there is a greater flexibility for the employer to deal with each situation on its individual merits. For example, in a small business, it will be almost impossible to lay down rules for when staff can change their hours to more flexible working practices as this will depend on factors such as the state and needs of the business and the general economy at that time. A non-contractual flexible working policy will not be prescriptive and can allow for the needs of the business to be accommodated.

The actual policies will vary depending on the nature of the business but common policies include:

- Disciplinary and Grievance Procedures (over and above the new statutory DDP and GP described in Chapter 2)
- Equal Opportunity policy
- Harassment policy
- E-mail and Internet policy
- Whistleblowing policy
- Parental leave and pay — maternity, paternity and adoption
- Flexible working policy
- Mobile telephone use policy
- Company car policy
- Telephone use policy
- Dress code policy
- Benefit schemes/bonus scheme rules
- Health and Safety policy
- Data Protection Act policy
- Expenses policy.

In Chapter 5 we deal with the use of in-house mediation and mediation as a means of resolving disputes. In order to utilise these techniques there should be a policy explaining when they will be used, how they will work, what will be done and by whom. By accepting the contract and staff handbook, staff will be accepting that in-house conciliation and mediation will be used to try and resolve disputes.

Whilst we think that there should be a policy covering in-house mediation there are different ways of dealing with this.

One way is to put a clause in the contract saying that all disputes (including both grievances and disciplinary) will be referred to in-house mediation. The advantage of this is that there is a simple commitment to in-house mediation and no need for a complex policy. The disadvantage is that the employer is bound to use in-house conciliation and mediation in all cases and this could be a cumbersome process in a case where the employee's guilt is clear.

Alternatively, a non-contractual policy could state that all disputes, including both grievances and disciplinary, will be referred to in-house mediation. This policy will be non contractual and so a failure to use in-house mediation will not be a breach of contract, although a failure to follow it will tend to show an unfair dismissal. In practice it may not be appropriate to use in-house mediation in disciplinary proceedings. If an employer needs to act quickly and decisively, in order to send a strong message to the workforce, having to arrange and hold an internal mediation will not achieve this.

A third option is to have a non-contractual policy that draws a distinction between grievance and disciplinary procedures and gives the employer flexibility when dealing with disciplinary procedures to decide whether the matter should go to mediation or not.

Many employers may prefer not to have a policy at all covering in-house and external mediation, as even though this is expressed to be discretionary, the discretion must be exercised fairly and uniformly. Therefore, if you used it for one member of staff and similar circumstances arise again but you do not apply the policy, this is likely to indicate unfair or discriminatory treatment. For an employer, it may be better to be aware of the concepts and to use them, if appropriate, but not to commit to using them. The strong disadvantage is that you cannot use the existence of a policy as evidence to a tribunal of how reasonable you are as an employer.

On balance we would advise that there is a non-contractual policy, which should allow as much flexibility as possible for disciplinary proceedings. In Chapter 4, the benefits of internal and external mediation in helping to resolve conflicts and disputes in the work place were discussed. The principles are not just there to be paid lip service as they might help defend an employment tribunal claim. Employers who embrace and adopt these techniques will, first and foremost, be creating a workplace in which conflict is managed and resolved effectively, allowing the business to focus on its core objectives of producing goods, selling products or providing services.

We now want to look in greater detail at the use of internal and external mediation in specific areas of conflict.

Grievance by Employee

In-house mediation is particularly useful here. The fact that an employee has a grievance shows that there is a conflict in the workplace. If it is not dealt with quickly and in an effective manner the conflict could easily escalate and lead to a claim against the employer. In such situations, having a policy to use in-house mediation will focus the manager's mind on resolving the problem. It will also show that the employer takes these issues very seriously and has acted reasonably in trying to resolve the problem.

Business Reorganisation/Redundancy

Again, the use of in-house mediation can play a very important role here in helping to manage the change process. If employees are being made redundant or having their terms and conditions of employment changed then they are likely to feel upset and aggrieved. If not handled properly this situation could escalate, in the worst case leading to an employment tribunal claim.

We think that management could use in-house mediation or external mediation as part of the redundancy or change procedure itself. Alternatively, and more usually, any problem employees can be identified quickly and then in-house mediation can be used to see whether the matter can be resolved amicably.

Disciplinary Investigation Against an Employee

In disciplinary cases, an employer is unlikely to want to be bound to refer the matter to an in-house mediator or external mediator. The employee has been caught red-handed and the commercial reality is for the employee to be disciplined quickly (provided that a fair investigation takes place and a fair procedure, including complying with the relevant DDP is followed). The employer does not want to be bound to try and resolve the matter.

Sample Clauses for a Contract

Grievance In the event of a dispute concerning the employee's employment, including any employee grievance, contractual dispute, or dispute arising from any change to your terms and conditions or a reorganisation, the parties agree that they shall first attempt to resolve the dispute themselves. Failing that, the parties agree that the matter may, at the absolute discretion of the employer, be dealt with in accordance with its in-house mediation policy for grievances, in which case the parties shall attempt to resolve the matter in good faith in accordance with that policy, provided that the parties agree that the policy does not form part of this contract of employment, and provided further that the parties shall not be precluded from seeking urgent injunctive or other relief from a court.
Disciplinary If, as part of any disciplinary proceedings against the employee, the employer in its absolute discretion considers that in-house mediation may be of assistance in resolving the problem, whether before or after a disciplinary decision has been taken, the parties agree that the matter may, at the absolute discretion of the employer, be dealt with in accordance with its mediation policy for disciplinary issues. In this case, the parties shall attempt to resolve the matter in good faith in accordance with that policy, provided that the parties agree that the policy does not form part of this contract of employment, and provided further that the parties shall not be precluded from seeking urgent injunctive or other relief from a court. For the avoidance of doubt, this clause does not give the employee the right to insist upon in-house mediation in any disciplinary case.

The policy itself should deal with issues such as who the mediator will be, what timescale will be involved for both employee and employer, a description of the procedure, what to expect and when the process can be ended by a party or by the mediator. It will also be vital to deal with the confidentiality of the in-house mediation, as this will be the employee's main concern. Before the in-house mediation takes place, all those involved should sign an agreement that specifically deals with confidentiality.

Sample confidentiality clause

1. The parties recognise and agree that the in-house mediation is for the purpose of attempting to resolve the dispute. In order to achieve this, both parties must be able to speak honestly and "put their cards on the table" and as such all information provided during the mediation is without prejudice and cannot be used in any litigation or arbitration of the dispute.
2. Evidence that is otherwise admissable shall not be rendered inadmissible as a result of its use in the in-house mediation. This means that if you produce evidence prior to the in-house mediation which helps your arguments, but it is not possible to resolve the dispute and the matter ends up before a court or tribunal, the use of that evidence during the mediation does not affect its use in court.
3. Any evidence that you produce during the in-house mediation can be used by you later on, but it cannot be used by the other side. Likewise, evidence gained by you from the other side during the in-house mediation may not later be used by you in a court or tribunal.
4. Neither of the parties may call nor require the mediator to give evidence about what was said at the mediation. All notes made by the mediator as part of the mediation (whether made before, during or after the mediation) will not be disclosed to any of the parties.
5. Every person involved in the mediation will keep confidential and not use for any collateral or ulterior purpose the fact that in-house mediation is to take place or has taken place.
6. All documents, statements, information and other material produced prior to or during the mediation, save to the extent that these documents have been disclosed already whether in writing or verbally, shall be held in strict confidence by the parties and shall be used solely for the purpose of the mediation.
7. At the end of the mediation all such material, and any copies of it, shall be returned to the originating party or immediately destroyed at their option.

Employees and Workers

The provisions of the Employment Act described in Chapter 2 apply to employees only. But what is an employee? How does that differ from a worker? The term worker has a wider definition. It can include self-employed contractors as well as people on secondments or placements.

The employment relationship is usually easy to recognise. You have an employer, an employee and a contract of employment exists between them. The employer gives the employee money and in return, the employee does the work that the employer gives him or her. However, there is a grey area where things are not so clear cut.

What if someone works three days a week in one place and two days somewhere else? What if they are labelled an independent contractor or consultant to avoid PAYE deductions from their pay?

Unfortunately, there is no one test that determines whether someone is an employee or not. In order to decide, an employment tribunal or court looks at the relationship as a whole. Therefore, there is no definitive guide, and you should take proper legal advice in each case. However, there are some core tests that indicate someone is an employee.

- Mutuality of obligation: if the company is obliged to offer work to the person and in return the person must accept it, they are likely to be an employee.
- Control: if the company exercises a high degree of control over what work the person does, when they do it and how they do it, that person is likely to be an employee.
- Means of payment: if tax and National Insurance are deducted under the PAYE scheme this indicates an employer/employee relationship.
- It is also important to look at the contract and see what the intention of the parties was, although the tribunal and court are allowed to disregard the label put on the relationship by the parties.

In the final analysis, the question of whether someone is or is not an employee really depends on the facts, and the overall view of the relationship.

What to Do When a Problem is Resolved

Where a dispute has been resolved and the employment relationship continues it is important that the agreement is recorded in writing so that it can be looked at in the future. In particular, there may be a degree of mistrust between employer and employee and this can be broken down with a clear and open statement of what will be done in the future and what changes will take place.

Usually an apology will build bridges like nothing else. A new contract should be issued if appropriate.

If the agreement reached is that the parties will go their separate ways amicably (or even when there is an ongoing, but varied, relationship) then the employer should consider a compromise agreement. This is a legally binding document that prevents an employee from starting or continuing employment tribunal claims. A compromise agreement should always be considered as it provides the certainty that a claim will not be brought or continued. It can also deal with ancillary matters such as any restrictions on the employee taking away clients, a confidentiality clause preventing the employee revealing the terms of the settlement and perhaps an agreement by the employer to give a reference.

In order for the agreement to be legally binding the employee must take independent legal advice on its terms and effect and it must be signed by the legal advisor. It is normal practice for the employer to make a contribution towards the employee's legal fees for getting this advice.

CHAPTER 7

Conclusion

The **Employment Act 2002** sets out a host of new employment rights and obligations. The central theme of many is to create a work environment in which disagreements can be freely aired and dealt with before parties become entrenched in their views and before the fundamental connection of trust and confidence that is critical to the employer-employee relationship breaks down.

The new rules, and particularly the statutory disciplinary and grievance procedures, are a starting point to identify disagreements at an early stage. However, the main failing of the new procedures is that they do not give any guidance or assistance on how to deal with the problem once it has been identified; it is largely left to the manager to deal with it as he or she sees fit. This can mean that the advantages of an early warning sign are lost if a manager handles the matter badly. In any event, as workplace disputes are often multi-factorial and involve complex dynamics and relationships, they require sensitive yet firm handling.

This guide sets out the benefits to a business in utilising mediation techniques to resolve disputes and ensure an efficient and effective workforce and suggested ways in which those techniques can be incorporated into existing disciplinary and grievance procedures.

From time to time there are problems that are best dealt with in a pragmatic manner. Mediation may not always be appropriate, but if it becomes recognised and trusted by both sides, then it can be a useful channel of communication with a view to putting the problem right, rather than one or other side scoring a victory. Of course, even if both sides agree on what the problem is, implementing the steps to rectify the situation can also be difficult. Here too the mediator can be valuable in maintaining the momentum for change and helping to decide a way forward.

INDEX

F

G

T

U

V

W